The Voice
of the Pe

HARRIS COUNTY PUBLIC LIBRARY

• 3 4028 05454 7006

331.097 Voi
The voice of the people :
  primary sources on the
  history of American
  labor, industrial relatio

$17.95
ocm52963283

D1490731

The Voice of the People

Primary Sources
on the History of American
Labor, Industrial Relations,
and Working-Class Culture

Jonathan Rees
Colorado State University—Pueblo
Jonathan Z. S. Pollack
Madison Area Technical College

Harlan Davidson, Inc.
Wheeling, Illinois 60090-6000

Copyright © 2004
Harlan Davidson, Inc.
All rights reserved.

Except as permitted under United States copyright law, no part of this
publication may be reproduced or distributed in any form or by any means,
or stored in a database or any retrieval system, without prior written permission of the publisher. Address inquiries to Harlan Davidson, Inc., 773 Glenn
Avenue, Wheeling, Illinois 60090-6000.

Visit us on the World Wide Web at www.harlandavidson.com.

Library of Congress Cataloging-in-Publication Data

The voice of the people: primary sources on the history of American labor,
industrial relations, and working-class culture / [compiled by] Jonathan Rees
and Jonathan Z. S. Pollack.
         p. cm.
    ISBN 0-88295-225-0 (alk. paper)
    1. Working class—United States—History—Sources. 2. Labor
unions—United States—History—Sources. I. Rees, Jonathan, 1966– II.
Pollack, Jonathan Z. S.
    HD8066.V65   2004
    331'.0973—dc22

                                                              2003018328

Cover photos (clockwise): Dairy Queen,1974, Wichita-Sedgwick County
Historical Museum; Homestead Riot, painting by W. P. Snyder, Walter P.
Reuther Library, Wayne State University; Mrs. Thomas with her maid, 1943,
Library of Congress, #LC-USW3-025238-D DLC; A worker carrying sugar cane,
Hilo, Hawaii, 1932, University of Chicago; Employees at Speedrite Products,
Inc., 1967, Archives of the Wichita Area Chamber of Commerce, Wichita State
University Library, Department of Special Collections.
Cover design: DePinto Graphic Design

Manufactured in the United States of America
06 05 04 1 2 3 VP

Contents

Acknowledgments

This book would not have been written without Andrew Davidson. He was interested in publishing it before we were certain we would write it. He has also helped us shape our vision of this work right down to its final stages. We have also received invaluable assistance from others at Harlan Davidson, especially Claudia Siler with permissions and Lucy Herz with production. Our friend David Zonderman of North Carolina State University shared his knowledge of labor history with us throughout our work on this project. He also got us interested in this subject in the first place by teaching our first labor history seminar. Thanks also to Steve McIntyre and Tom Dicke of Southwest Missouri State University, Roger Horowitz of the Hagley Museum and Library, Lynda DeLoach of the George Meany Memorial Archives, and Peter Gilmore of the United Electrical Workers. The archives and library reference staff of the Wisconsin Historical Society, especially Andy Kraushaar and Rick Pifer, provided invaluable assistance.

J.R.
J.Z.S.P.

Introduction

THE FIRST THING you should know about this book is that it includes only primary sources. Whether personal in nature, such as correspondence or journal entries, or public, such as speeches or newspaper or magazine articles, primary sources are words written at or around the time of a particular historical event by participants or direct observers. This distinguishes them from secondary sources, materials written after the event in question has passed into history. In many cases, historical actors are the authors of primary sources, while historians usually write secondary sources. We believe that students studying any field of history benefit from exposure to a wide range of primary sources because this gives them the ability to see history through the perspective of persons who were there. Primary sources also show students the origin of secondary sources, including the interpretations found in their textbooks. This is fundamental for understanding how historians do their work.

Primary sources are particularly useful for understanding American labor history because working people always have and always will see their history differently than scholars far removed from the world of wage labor. Many labor history scholars bring particularly strong points of view towards their subject matter. And while we admit to having strong views of our own on this topic, we want students to form their own opinions about labor history.

In selecting pieces to excerpt for this volume, we made every effort to include as many working-class voices as possible.

This was not easy. Over the course of American history, few working-class people recorded their feelings or experiences in writing. This likely was a function of their relatively limited education and access to mass media and, perhaps most important, their disinclination to write. Indeed, persons working twelve or more hours a day probably had more pressing things to do when they got home than scribbling in a journal or firing off an angry letter to the editor of the local newspaper. Therefore, we had no choice but to include a number of pieces written by people who were/are not of the working class. While the impressions of journalists, scholars—even managers—may not tell us what the working class thought, they can help us understand the conditions workers endured and the opinions they formed. Scholars often read between the lines of sources like these to understand the actions of "voiceless" people.

We also deliberately chose to keep the length of the excerpts in this volume short, principally because we want student readers to experience the full variety of the source materials we present. In addition, we fully expect instructors to use this book in conjunction with other assigned materials, especially textbooks on American labor history. This book offers instructors and students an affordable and accessible alternative to expensive, lengthy supplements that many students have difficulty reading, especially within the time constraints of a single-semester course.

Because most textbooks are organized chronologically, we did not deviate far from that approach. We have divided this book into four parts: To 1877, 1877 to 1914, 1914 to 1945, and 1945 to the Present. We have classified each selected reading into one of these parts based on when the event described occurred, rather than when the document was written. While the years these partitions comprise are not necessarily significant to the history of American labor, they do reflect general dividing lines in American history, which in turn affected the directions American labor took. World War II, for example, increased employment, so the issues facing laborers after the war were vastly different from those prominent during the Great Depression, before the war began. Each of the four parts begins with a short essay in which we seek to put the events the labor documents describe into the context of general American history during the given period. Within each of the four chronological parts, the documents are classified under one of three categories: Work and Labor / Management Relations; The Union Movement; and Working-Class Culture.

Throughout American history, labor and management have struggled over the definition of labor's specific duties and responsibilities. Materials describing these conflicts appear in the Work and Labor / Management Relations subsections, as do sources that describe exactly what workers did all day, some in the words of the workers themselves. Some of these selections describe difficult working conditions no longer tolerated in modern America; sadly, others are testament to difficult working conditions modern America spawned.

The Union Movement refers to the history of worker organization in the United States. These sections include material on organizing efforts, collective bargaining and, of course, strikes. Studying the union movement has become unfashionable in labor history circles in recent years. Compared to unions in other countries, labor organizations in the United States have been very conservative, seldom challenging their employers for a bigger share of the pie. This has led to severe problems over the last few decades, as employers have become bolder in their attempts to eliminate unions from their shops entirely. Therefore, many labor historians have focused on unorganized workers in order to demonstrate that gains for workers are possible even in the absence of traditional collective bargaining.

Nevertheless, we chose to devote a large amount of space to the Union Movement sections. First, even though trade union members have never made up a majority of the American working class, they have been particularly important to the course of American labor history. For example, employers have tended to match union contract terms for their non-union workers in order to make outside unions less appealing. Second, the union movement has served as the political voice of the American working class over the course of American labor history, thereby magnifying its significance beyond the size of its membership. Finally, we gave considerable space to the union movement because we believe that its history reflects on both the past and the present. Understanding its failure helps explain why so many workers in the past were not union members. It can also provide lessons for modern trade unionists facing the same kinds of problems today. Since many political interests have grown increasingly hostile towards organized labor in recent years, these lessons may prove increasingly valuable.

Sources classified under the Working-Class Culture sections convey beliefs workers held and activities they practiced to give their lives meaning. For historians, working-class culture is most clearly visible outside the workplace, where laborers were free from the obvious influence of employers. Much of the material in these groupings refers to family life, but it also covers what workers did when they got together off the job, like going to the saloon or the theater. The importance of working-class culture derives in large part from the size of the working class. One can even argue that working-class culture is the basis of our modern mass culture, for the majority of modern cultural consumers are employees. Working-class culture is also important because it has often been an expression of militancy and a cause of class conflict.

We recognize that the categories we present are in many ways arbitrary. For example, cultural issues often reflected on labor management relations and vice versa. To compensate for this, we suggest that instructors assign sections in any order they see fit.

Three questions follow each of the documents in this reader. The purpose of these questions is not to test reading comprehension, but to help student readers place what they have read into the context of other labor struggles, both historical and contemporary. Because there are no right answers to these questions, we hope they provoke individual thought and classroom discussion.

Unlike some other branches of history, labor history is a particularly personal enterprise. Relatively few Americans ever become a prominent politician or a famous historical figure, but almost all Americans have to work at some point in their lives. We believe that reading the primary sources excerpted in this book will not only deepen your understanding of American history, but that of your own past, present, and future. The struggle between labor and management has proved to be a constant in American life. Therefore, what you read in this book may be among the most useful and resonant information you receive in the course of your education.

Jonathan Rees
Colorado State University—Pueblo
Jonathan Z. S. Pollack
Madison Area Technical College

Part I: To 1877

THE MOST IMPORTANT and difficult problem facing early America was a shortage of labor. Few skilled workers came to the New World. They had no reason to risk migration when demand for their skills existed at home. But even the demand for less-skilled workers in the American colonies outstripped supply. Without labor, no one could use the rich natural resources of the New World to better their economic standing and justify migration in the first place.

There were many reasons for this labor shortage. Immigration to the New World was difficult before 1800. Passage was expensive and dangerous. European immigrants suffered high death rates once they arrived. Since British immigrants in mainland North America failed to find easy money through gold mining or sugar production, there was not a lot to pull them them there at first. But the most vexing reason of all for the shortage was the desire of workers already there to work for themselves, so that they might become rich too. People who worked for somebody else were unable to benefit from the high price of tobacco or the intense demand for shoemakers or barrel-making in growing New England villages. Employers would keep the lion's share of the profits, even while workers put out most of the effort.

In the very first stages of settlement, workers had to join together with their neighbors so that their colonies could survive (see number 1, Bradford). In later decades, as communities in America became more established and joined together to form colonies, people began to work for themselves. Because there was so much available, good-quality land, many settlers who could labor for themselves could make lots of money.

For example, the tidewater areas of Virginia and Maryland were perfect for growing tobacco. During most of the 1600s, tobacco prices were so high that few people in Virginia and Maryland wanted to grow anything else. Tobacco could make a man a fortune, but a successful tobacco farmer could not make a fortune by himself. Tobacco cultivation was extremely labor-intensive. It took nine months of hard work to grow it and more work after that to cultivate it and prepare the land for the next year's crop. This harsh regimen made it less likely that anyone would want to do this kind of work for someone else.

English settlers in America devised a variety of methods to control labor. Early Virginians wanted to induce local Native American tribes to work for them. When this proved too difficult, they turned to indentured servants shipped from the mother country. Most indentured servants came from the ranks of London's poor, and many of them were actually orphans who were forced to work in exchange for their passage (see number 2, Jones). The most fortunate young male workers were taken on as apprentices, taught a marketable skill, and allowed to practice their trade for pay once they came of age (see number 6, Otter).

Most northern workers were neither indentured servants nor apprentices. They were part of a family economy, in which men and women toiled the land together to scratch out a comfortable but not luxurious existence. If such a farm produced more than enough to feed the family, they might trade or sell its goods on the open market. Some northerners succeeded through buying and selling the products of the land. While some families got by through subsistence agriculture, others became victims of tragedies like disease, bad weather, or war.

After 1660, Southern colonies came to rely on enslaved labor from Africa. These workers did not migrate willingly. They were kidnapped and transported to the New World to provide labor at no wage. At first, they mostly grew tobacco. After 1800, Southerners used most of their slaves to grow cotton (see number 3, Ball) another crop that Europeans desperately wanted. Most of that cotton went to English textile mills, which were just then beginning to develop into large factories.

Beginning in the early nineteenth century, industrialization began to change the picture for countless American workers too. Now workers were brought together in large factories, and set upon repetitive tasks. They were also paid a wage for their labor, something that was quite rare in the American economy before that time. Factory work was even open to women (see number 4, Farley), especially in the burgeoning textile towns of New England.

Skilled workers were hurt by these developments. The changes in work processes, particularly the widespread use of machines, often rendered their talents obsolete because cheap competition for their products could drive them out of business. These conditions led skilled workers to form the first unions in the United States (see number 7, Manning, and number 8, "Recruiting Song"). By the 1860s, when the demand for soldiers to fight the Civil War caused a severe labor shortage, unions had become a permanent fixture in the American economy. Even though they only represented a minority of workers, unions could exercise significant power over politics through their effects on the economy. For example, they made legislation for shorter working hours one of the most important political issues of the late nineteenth century (see number 9, Phillips).

Faced with low pay, long hours, and badly limited prospects for advancement, workers began to commiserate among themselves in order to brighten their often-drab lives. Singing was one way to achieve this cultural solidarity (see number 8, "Recruiting Song"). Unions did much to perpetuate this kind of working-class culture. Cigar rollers, for example, used to have one worker read aloud to his fellow union members so that their workday would go faster (see number 12, Gompers). Even without a union or without pay, American workers needed a way to let off steam. In 1849, New York's working class showed its cultural solidarity against the English actor William Charles Macready during the Astor Place Riot (see number 11, "Astor Place Riot"). The benefit of working-class culture was not limited to white male workers. For example, despite their difficult circumstances, slaves were able to carve out areas of their lives that they could control so as to give them satisfaction (see number 13, Keckley). By the time of the Civil War, the culture of the American working class was visible everywhere (see number 14, Burn).

Although American workers benefited from lower prices on consumer goods, the pace of industrialization during this period hurt many workers at the same time. As more industries used technology to improve production, more and more people found that the skills they possessed were obsolete. And while the early phase of industrialization affected skilled workers the most, this later stage adversely affected workers of all kinds. In the Northeast, unskilled workers increasingly found themselves competing for jobs with immigrants from Eastern and Southern Europe. In the West, many of the immigrants were Asian (see number 5, Twain). Generally, all of these recent immigrants were willing to accept lower pay and work longer hours than native-born Americans, which allowed employers to demand longer hours for less pay from all workers.

Improvements in working conditions and the success of unions during the war years gave American workers a sense of rising expectations. Once the war ended and hard times hit, American workers and their employers would fight ever more frequently over the difficult conditions that industrialization created.

Work and Labor/ Management Relations

Winslow Homer drawing depicting workers streaming out of the textile mills of Lowell, Massachusetts, 1860s. Courtesy of George Meany Memorial Archives.

1

William Bradford Recounts the Social Development of Plymouth Plantation, ca. 1647

Jamestown, founded in 1607, in what became Virginia, was the first permanent English colony in mainland North America. The first group of settlers there hoped to find gold or other means of getting rich quick. Among their number were jewelers, perfumers, and other gentlemen of leisure. Many lacked the necessary skills, even the will, to survive in this new land, let alone transform it into a thriving colony.

Protestant dissenters, known now as Pilgrims, fled religious perse-cution to found Plymouth, the second permanent English colony, in 1620. They, too, faced the immediate problem of finding food, yet they embarked upon collective hunting and gathering to sustain themselves. Soon thereafter, with the help of local American Indians who showed them how to cultivate native crops, the Plymouth colonists practiced collective agriculture.

William Bradford served as governor of Plymouth, Massachusetts, from 1620 until his death in 1657. He determined that this form of communal labor stymied overall production and failed to reward an individual's hard work and initiative. Here, in his memoir of early Ply-mouth, Bradford describes how in 1623 he remedied this situation by rearranging the agricultural system so that settlers worked for them-selves. Bradford, like most of his fellow colonists, was deeply religious. Therefore, he assumed that his new arrangement, which helped some at the expense of others, was God's will.

ALL THIS WHILE NO supply was heard of, neither knew they when they might expecte any. So they begane to thinke how they might

Excerpt from William Bradford, *History of Plymouth Plantation*, (Boston: Mass-achusetts Historical Society, 1856), 134–36. The authors of this reader have edited the typesetting of this excerpt to modern standards; spelling and style are original.

raise as much corne as they could, and obtaine a better crope
than they had done, that they might not thus still languish in
miserie. At length, after much debate of things, the Gov[ernor]
(with ye advice of the chiefest among them) gave way that they
should set corne every man for his owne perticuler, and in that
regard trust to them selves; in all other things to goe on in ye
general way as before. And so assigned to every family a parcell
of land, according to proportion of their number for that end,
only the present use (but made no devission for inheritance),
and ranged all boys & youths under some familie. This had very
good success; for it made all hands very industrious, so as much
corne was planted then other waise would have bene by any
means ye Gover[ernor] or any other could use, and saved him a
great deall of trouble, and gave farr better contente. The women
now wente willingly into ye feild, and tooke their little-ons with
them to set corne, which before would aledg weaknes, and
inabilitie; whom to have compelled would have bene thought great
tiranie and oppression.

The experience that was had in this comone course and condition, tried sundrie years, and that amongst godly and sober men,
may will evince the vanity of that conceit of Platos* & other an-
cients applauded by some of later times; that ye taking away
of propertie and bringing in community into a commonwealth
would make them happy and flourishing; as if they were wiser
than God. For this communitie (so farr as it was) was found to
breed much confusion & discontent, and retard much [employ-
ment] that would have been to their benefite and comforte. For
ye yong-men that were most able and fit for labour & service did
repine that they should spend their time & strength to worke for
other mens wives and children without any recompence. The
strong, or man of parts, had no more in devission of [food] &
clothes than he that was weake and not able to doe a quarter ye
other could; this was thought injuestice. The aged and graver
men to be ranked and . . . equalised in labours and [food], cloathes,
[etc.], with ye meaner & yonger sorte, thought it some indignitie
and disrespect unto them. And for mens wives to be commanded

---

*Plato: Ancient Greek philosopher and author of *The Republic,* a book that
describes a communal arrangement as ideal for the government of man.

to doe service for other men, as dressing their meate, washing their clothes, [etc.], they deemd it a kind of slaverie, neither could many husbands well brooke it. Upon ye poynte all being to have alike, and all to doe alike, they thought them selves in ye like condition, and one as good as another; and so, if it did not cut off those relations that God hath set amongest men, yet it did at least much diminish and take of ye mutual respects that should be preserved amongst them. And would have been worse if they had been men of another condition. Let none objecte this is men's corruption, and nothing to ye course it selfe. I answer, seeing all men have this corruption in them, God in his wisdome saw another course fiter for them.

QUESTIONS

1. Explain the traits of the "common course and condition." What kind of social arrangement replaced it after it ended?
2. Do you agree with Bradford that this change was good for Plymouth? Explain.
3. Do you see a relationship between the creation of private land and the later creation of the working and capitalist classes in America?

2

Hugh Jones on White Indentured Servitude in Virginia, 1724

England conceived of the system of indentured servitude as a way to control idle poor people who teemed into its cities during the 1500s and 1600s. The English poor worked long hours in bad conditions in order to avoid starvation or imprisonment. When America opened up to settlement, English authorities saw a way to kill two birds with one stone. Indenturing servants to work in America meant fewer poor people in England where they were unwanted, and more in the American colonies, where their labor was desperately needed.

Here, Hugh Jones, writing in a guide to the state of Virginia intended for Englishmen who knew little of this far-off colony, describes three kinds of labor: contract labor, indentured servitude, and convict labor. No workers in these categories could move to work for themselves or even sell their labor to the highest bidder, because the law compelled them to help their masters become rich. Of these kinds of laborers, indentured servants were most prevalent. These workers bound themselves to a particular master for a set period of time in return for the cost of their passage to America and the hope of making a new start after their terms of indenture expired. By Jones's time, indentured servitude was dying out because an increasing number of

Excerpt from Hugh Jones, "Present State of Virginia, 1724," in John R. Commons, ed., *Documentary History of Industrial Society*, Vol. I (Cleveland: A. H. Clark Co., 1910–1911), 339–40. The authors of this reader have edited the typesetting of this excerpt to modern standards; spelling and style are original.

landowners preferred to buy slaves, whom they could control for their entire natural lives. The mention of "Negroes" in the last sentence here is a reminder that some Africans were subject to servitude rather than slavery even at this late date.

THE SHIPS THAT TRANSPORT these Things often call at Ireland to victual, and bring over frequently white Servants, which are of three Kinds. 1. Such as come upon certain Wages by Agreement for a certain Time. 2. Such as come bound by Indenture, commonly call'd Kids, who are usually to serve four or five Years; and 3. those Convicts or Felons that are transported, whose Room they had much rather have than their Company; for abundance of them do great Mischiefs, commit robbery and Murder, and spoil Servants, that were before very good: But they frequently there meet with the end they deserved at Home, though indeed some of them prove indifferent good. Their being sent thither to work as Slaves for Punishment, is but a mere Notion, for few of them ever lived so well and so easy before, especially if they are good for any thing. These are to serve seven and sometimes fourteen Years, and they and Servants by indentures have an Allowance of Corn and Cloaths, when they are out of their Time, that they may be therewith supported, till they can be provided with Services, or otherwise settled. With these three sorts of Servants are they supplied from England, Wales, Scotland and Ireland, among which they have a Mind to it may serve their Time with Ease and Satisfaction to themselves and their Masters, especially if they fall into good Hands.

Except the last Sort, for the most Part who are loose Villains, made tame by Wild, and then enslaved by his Forward Namesake: To prevent too great a Stock of which Servants, and Negroes many Attempts and Laws have been in vain made.

These if they forsake their Roguery together with the other Kids . . . when they are free, may work Day-Labour, or else rent a small Plantation for a Trifle almost; or else turn Overseers, if they are expert, industrious and careful, or follow their Trade, if they have been brought up to any; especially Smiths, Carpenters, Taylors, Sawyers, Coopers, Bricklayers, &c. The Plenty of the Country and the good Wages given to Work-Folks occasion very few Poor, who are supported by the Parish, being such as are

lame, sick or decrepit through Age, Distempers, Accidents, or
some Infirmities; for where there is a numerous Family of poor
Children the Vestry takes care to bind them out Apprentices, till
they are able to maintain themselves by their own Labour; by
which Means they are never tormented with Vagrant, and Vaga-
bond Beggars, there being a Reward for taking up Runaways, that
are a small Distance from their Home; if they are not known or
without a Pass from their Master, and can give no good Account
of themselves, especially Negroes. . . .

QUESTIONS

1. From the servant's perspective, do any of these three types of
   servitude seem like a good deal?
2. From the perspective of the residents of Virginia, do these
   kinds of servitude seem like a good deal?
3. What are the similarities and differences between indentured
   servants and slaves?

3 ──────────────────────────────

Charles Ball Describes a Typical Day on a Slave Plantation

Slavery in the United States began during the colonial period as a labor system for shorthanded Southern landowners. Over time, the planters' need for labor interwined with race prejudice to make slaves economically and socially subservient. Slaves were used to fulfill many tasks, but perhaps the most brutal work was reserved for those forced to toil in the cotton fields of large plantations.

Charles Ball was one of many former slaves who escaped slavery, but one of the comparatively few of these individuals who could or did write about his experiences in bondage. Here Ball describes what he experienced as a typical day at work on a large Southern slave plantation during the mid-nineteenth century.

As I HAVE BEFORE stated, there were altogether on this plantation, two hundred and sixty slaves; but the number was seldom stationary for a single week. Births were numerous and frequent, and deaths were not uncommon. When I joined them I believe we counted in all two hundred and sixty-three; but of these only one hundred and seventy went to the field to work. The others were children, too small to be of any service as laborers; old and blind persons, or incurably diseased. Ten or twelve were kept about the mansion-house and garden, chosen from the most handsome and sprightly of the gang.

Excerpt from Charles Ball, *Fifty Years in Chains or, the Life of an American Slave* (New York: H. Dayton, 1859), 117–122. The spelling is original.

I think about one hundred and sixty-eight assembled this morning, at the sound of the horn—two or three being sick, sent word to the overseer that they could not come.

The overseer wrote something on a piece of paper, and gave it to his little son. This I was told was a note to be sent to our master, to inform him that some of the hands were sick—it not being any part of the duty of the overseer to attend to a sick negro.

The overseer then led off to the field, with his horn in one hand and his whip in the other; we following—men, women, and children, promiscuously—and a wretched looking troop we were. There was not an entire garment amongst us.

More than half of the gang were entirely naked. Several young girls, who had arrived at puberty, wearing only the livery with which nature had ornamented them, and a great number of lads, of an equal or superior age, appeared in the same costume. There was neither bonnet, cap, nor head dress of any kind amongst us, except the old straw hat that I wore, and which my wife had made for me in Maryland. This I soon laid aside to avoid the appearance of singularity, and, as owing to the severe treatment I had endured whilst traveling in chains, and being compelled to sleep on the naked floor, without undressing myself, my clothes were quite worn out, I did not make a much better figure than my companions; though still I preserved the semblance of clothing so far, that it could be seen that my shirt and trowsers had once been distinct and separate garments. Not one of the others had on even the remains of two pieces of apparel.—Some of the men had old shirts, and some ragged trowsers, but no one wore both. Amongst the women, several wore petticoats, and many had shifts. Not one of the whole number wore both of these vestments.

We walked nearly a mile through one vast cotton field, before we arrived at the place of our intended day's labor. At last the overseer stopped at the side of the field, and calling to several of the men by name, ordered them to call their companies and turn into their rows. The work we had to do today was to hoe and weed cotton, for the last time; and the men whose names had been called, and who were, I believe, eleven in number, were designated as captains, each of whom had under his command a certain number of the other hands. The captain was the foreman of his company, and those under his command had to keep up with him. Each of the men and women had to take one row; and two, and in some cases where they were very small, three of the children had one. The first captain, whose name was Simon, took the first row—and the other captains were compelled to keep up with him. By this means the overseer had nothing to do but to keep Simon hard at work, and he was certain that all the others must work equally hard.

Simon was a stout, strong man, apparently about thirty-five years of age; and for some reason unknown to me, I was ordered to take a row next to his. The overseer with his whip in his hand walked about the field after us, to see that our work was well done. As we worked with hoes, I had no difficulty in learning how the work was to be performed.

The fields of cotton at this season of the year are very beautiful. The plants, among which we worked this day, were about three feet high, and in full bloom, with branches so numerous that they nearly covered the whole ground—leaving scarcely space enough between them to permit us to move about, and work with our hoes. . . .

When we could no longer see to work, the horn was again sounded, and we returned home. I had now lived through one of the days—a successsion of which make up the life of a slave —on a cotton plantation.

QUESTIONS

1. In what manner did the overseer make sure that all the slaves present worked hard throughout the long day?
2. Do you think it might have paid off in the long run for Ball's owner to have fed and clothed his slaves better?
3. Do you think Ball is a trustworthy source for describing the circumstances of slaves in the cotton fields? Why or why not?

4

Harriet Farley, "Letter From Susan," 1844

Industrialization involves two related trends: mechanization—the replacement of men with machines—and the division of labor—bringing workers together under one roof and breaking down their tasks into small parts in order to eliminate inefficiency. Industrialization in the United States began around 1820. As a result, production in the American economy increased sharply, and the nature of work changed forever.

Textile making was among the first industries in the United States to become industrialized. New England textile firms used British technological innovations and a largely female workforce to expand during the early to mid-nineteenth century. Lowell, Massachusetts, a town built by a group of wealthy families and investors known as the Boston Associates in 1820, grew to become the largest textile-manufacturing center in the world.

Unlike many other workers, the women of Lowell saw fit to start their own literary magazine, The Lowell Offering. *The magazine was intended to counter widespread prejudice against working-class mill girls. The writing it contained offers a unique perspective on the "Lowell Mill Girls," their working conditions, and worker's lives. Harriet Farley was one of the* Offering's *editors. Although this and her "Letters from Susan" are technically fiction, they are closely based on experiences and attitudes that Farley and her readers encountered every day in the mills.*

Excerpt from *The Lowell Offering*, Volume 4, 1844.

LETTER SECOND

Lowell, April —, ——

Dear Mary: In my last I told you I would write again, and say more of my life here; and this I will now attempt to do.

I went into the mill to work a few days after I wrote to you. It looked very pleasant at first, the rooms were so light, spacious, and clean, the girls so pretty and neatly dressed, and the machinery so brightly polished or nicely painted. The plants in the windows, or on the overseer's bench or desk, gave a pleasant aspect to things. You will wish to know what work I am doing. I will tell you of the different kinds of work.

There is, first, the carding-room, where the cotton flies most, and the girls get the dirtiest. But this is easy, and the females are allowed time to go out at night before the bell rings—on Saturday night at least, if not on all other nights. Then there is the spinning-room, which is very neat and pretty. In this room are the spinners and doffers. The spinners watch the frames; keep them clean, and the threads mended if they break. The doffers take off the full bobbins, and put on the empty ones. They have nothing to do in the long intervals when the frames are in motion, and can go out to their boarding-houses, or do any thing else that they like. In some of the factories the spinners do their own doffing, and when this is the case they work no harder than the weavers. These last have the hardest time of all—or can have, if they choose to take charge of three or four looms, instead of the one pair which is the allotment. And they are the most constantly confined. The spinners and dressers have but the weavers to keep supplied, and then their work can stop. The dressers never work before breakfast, and they stay out a great deal in the afternoons. The drawers-in, or girls who draw the threads through the harnesses, also work in the dressing-room, and they all have very good wages—better than the weavers who have but the usual work. The dressing-rooms are very neat, and the frames move with a gentle undulating motion which is really graceful. But these rooms are kept very warm, and are disagreeably scented with the "sizing," or starch, which stiffens the "beams," or unwoven webs. There are many plants in these rooms, and it is really a good green-house for them. The dressers are generally quite tall girls, and must have

pretty tall minds too, as their work requires much care and attention.

I could have had work in the dressing-room, but chose to be
a weaver; and I will tell you why. I disliked the closer air of the
dressing-room, though I might have become accustomed to that.
I could not learn to dress so quickly as I could to weave, nor have
work of my own so soon, and should have had to stay with Mrs.
C. two or three weeks before I could go in at all, and I did not like
to be "lying upon my oars" so long. And, more than this, when I
get well learned I can have extra work, and make double wages,
which you know is quite an inducement with some.

Well, I went into the mill, and was put to learn with a very
patient girl—a clever old maid. I should be willing to be one myself if I could be as good as she is. You cannot think how odd
every thing seemed to me. I wanted to laugh at every thing, but
did not know what to make sport of first. They set me to threading shuttles, and tying weaver's knots, and such things, and now
I have improved so that I can take care of one loom. I could take
care of two if I only had eyes in the back part of my head, but I
have not got used to "looking two ways of a Sunday" yet.

At first the hours seemed very long, but I was so interested
in learning that I endured it very well; and when I went out at
night the sound of the mill was in my ears, as of crickets, frogs,
and jewsharps, all mingled together in strange discord. After that
it seemed as though cotton-wool was in my ears, but now I do not
mind at all. You know that people learn to sleep with the thunder
of Niagara in their ears, and a cotton mill is no worse, though you
wonder that we do not have to hold our breath in such a noise.

It makes my feet ache and swell to stand so much, but I
suppose I shall get accustomed to that too. The girls generally
wear old shoes about their work, and you know nothing is easier;
but they almost all say that when they have worked here a year
or two they have to procure shoes a size or two larger than before
they came. The right hand, which is the one used in stopping
and starting the loom, becomes larger than the left; but in other
respects the factory is not detrimental to a young girl's appearance. Here they look delicate, but not sickly; they laugh at those
who are much exposed, and get pretty brown; but I, for one, had

rather be brown than pure white. I never saw so many pretty looking girls as there are here. Though the number of men is small in proportion there are many marriages here, and a great deal of courting. I will tell you of this last sometime.

You wish to know minutely of our hours of labor. We go in at five o'clock; at seven we come out to breakfast; at half-past seven we return to our work, and stay until half-past twelve. At one, or quarter-past one four months in the year, we return to our work, and stay until seven at night. Then the evening is all our own, which is more than some laboring girls can say, who think nothing is more tedious than a factory life.

When I first came here, which was the last of February, the girls ate their breakfast before they went to their work. The first of March they came out at the present breakfast hour, and the twentieth of March they ceased to "light up" the rooms, and come out between six and seven o'clock.

You ask if the girls are contented here: I ask you, if you know of any one who is perfectly contented. Do you remember the old story of the philosopher, who offered a field to the person who was contented with his lot; and, when one claimed it, he asked him why, if he was so perfectly satisfied, he wanted his field. The girls here are not contented; and there is no disadvantage in their situation which they do not perceive as quickly, and lament as loudly, as the sternest opponents of the factory system do. They would scorn to say they were contented, if asked the question; for it would compromise their Yankee spirit—their pride, penetration, independence, and love of "freedom and equality" to say that they were contented with such a life as this. Yet, withal, they are cheerful. I never saw a happier set of beings. They appear blithe in the mill, and out of it. If you see one of them, with a very long face, you may be sure that it is because she has heard bad news from home, or because her beau has vexed her. But, if it is a Lowell trouble, it is because she has failed in getting off as many "sets" or "pieces" as she intended to have done; or because she had a sad "break-out," or "break-down," in her work, or something of that sort.

You ask if the work is not disagreeable. Not when one is accustomed to it. It tried my patience sadly at first, and does now when it does not run well; but, in general, I like it very much. It is easy to do, and does not require very violent exertion, as much of our farm work does. . . .

Yours as ever, Susan

QUESTIONS

1. How does "Susan's" gender affect the way she views her job?
2. Why does "Susan" seem to like the work even if the other girls do not?
3. Does your interpretation of the letter change knowing it is fiction rather than an actual letter? What might have been Harriet Farley's reasons for writing it?

5

Mark Twain on the Chinese Population of Virginia City, Nevada, 1872

Before the publication of his best-selling novels Tom Sawyer *and* The Adventures of Huckleberry Finn, *the author known as Mark Twain wrote essays inspired by his travels in the American West. In two compilations of essays first published in 1872,* Roughing It *and* The Innocents at Home, *Twain describes the West he experienced and cleverly, if cynically, pokes fun at American ideals and the reality of American life.*

In this selection, Twain takes issue with the movement to restrict Chinese immigration to the United States, which was one of the first successful lobbying efforts by the American Federation of Labor. In sketching out this early generation of Chinese Americans, Twain is at once a man of his time in his stereotypes of Chinese workers, and ahead of it in his mocking of the pro-exclusionary argument.

OF COURSE THERE WAS a large Chinese population in Virginia [City, Nevada]—it is the case with every town and city on the Pacific coast. They are a harmless race when white men either let them alone or treat them no worse than dogs; in fact they are almost entirely harmless anyhow, for they seldom think of resenting the vilest insults or the cruellest injuries. They are quiet, peaceable, tractable, free from drunkenness, and they are industrious as the day is long. A disorderly Chinaman is rare, and a lazy one

Excerpt from Mark Twain [Samuel Langhorne Clemens], *The Innocents at Home* (London: George Routledge and Sons, Limited, 1872), 65–67, 70–71.

does not exist. So long as a Chinaman has strength to use his hands he needs no support from anybody; white men often complain of want of work, but a Chinaman offers no such complaint; he always manages to find something to do. He is a great convenience to everybody—even to the worst class of white men, for he bears the most of their sins, suffering fines for their petty thefts, imprisonment for their robberies, and death for their murders. Any white man can swear a Chinaman's life away in the courts, but no Chinaman can testify against a white man. Ours is "the land of the free"—nobody denies that—nobody challenges it. (Maybe it is because we won't let other people testify.) As I write, news comes that in broad daylight in San Francisco, some boys have stoned an inoffensive Chinaman to death, and that although a large crowd witnessed the shameful deed, no one interfered.

There are seventy thousand (and quite possibly one hundred thousand) Chinamen on the Pacific coast. There were about a thousand in Virginia. They were penned into a "Chinese quarter"—a thing which they do not particularly object to, as they are fond of herding together. Their buildings were made of wood; usually only one storey high, and set through. Their quarter was a little removed from the rest of the town. The chief employment of Chinamen in towns is to wash clothing. They always send a bill pinned to the clothes. It is mere ceremony, for it does not enlighten the customer much. Their price for washing was $2.50 per dozen—rather cheaper than white people could afford to wash for at that time. A very common sign on the Chinese houses was: "See Yup, Washer and Ironer;" "Hung Wo, Washer;" "Sam Sing & Ah Hop, Washing." The house servants, cooks, etc., in California and Nevada, were chiefly Chinamen. There were few white servants and no China-women were employed. Chinamen make good house servants, being quick, obedient, patient, quick to learn, and tirelessly industrious. They do not need to be taught a thing twice, as a general thing. They are imitative. If a Chinaman were to see his master break up a centre table, in a passion, and kindle a fire with it, that Chinaman would be likely to resort to the furniture for fuel for ever afterward.

All Chinamen can read, write, and cipher with easy facility—pity but our petted voters could. In California they rent little patches of ground, and do a great deal of gardening. They will raise surprising crops of vegetables on a sand pile. They waste nothing. What is rubbish to a Christian, a Chinaman carefully preserves and makes useful in one way or another. He gathers up all the old oyster and sardine cans that white people throw away, and procures marketable tin and solder from them by melting. He gathers up old bones and turns them into manure. In California he gets a living out of old mining claims that white men have abandoned as exhausted and worthless—and then the officers come down on him once a month with an exorbitant swindle to which the legislature has given the broad, general name of "foreign" mining tax, but it is usually inflicted on no foreigners but Chinamen. This swindle has in some cases been repeated once or twice on the same victim in the course of the same month—but the public treasury was not additionally enriched by it, probably.

. . . They are a kindly disposed, well-meaning race, and are respected and well treated by the upper classes, all over the Pacific coast. No Californian *gentleman* or *lady* ever abuses or oppresses a Chinaman, under any circumstances, an explanation that seems to be much needed in the east. Only the scum of the population do it—they and their children; they and, naturally and consistently, the policemen and politicians likewise, for these are the dust-licking pimps and slaves of the scum, there as well as elsewhere in America.

Questions

1. Which parts of this essay show Twain's sympathy with Chinese workers trying to make a living in western mining towns? To what extent does Twain reinforce negative images of Chinese workers?

2. How would you explain Virginia City's Chinese workers' ability to get by on less money and amenities than their white counterparts?

3. After reading this essay, why do you think groups like the American Federation of Labor favored Chinese exclusion?

The Union Movement

Membership certificate for the United Order of Mechanics, 1848.
Courtesy of Public Affairs Press.

6

William Otter Recalls His Unsuccessful Career as an Apprentice, 1835

Apprenticeship was a labor system that dated back to medieval times. In it, skilled workers would take in young men, often their sons, and teach them their trade during which time the apprentices worked for little or no compensation. Usually, this arrangement was enforced through a legal contract between master and apprentice. The masters got cheap labor, while the apprentices learned skills that allowed them to start their own businesses one day. Both parties benefited by limiting the knowledge of these skills to a small number of people. In this way, tradesmen could expect to face little competition for their services so they could keep the fees their customers paid high.

William Otter was one of the few nineteenth-century tradesmen who wrote an autobiography. Although he became a successful plasterer, here he describes his experience looking for an apprenticeship. The variety of jobs he tried suggests the difficulty of skilled labor at this time. The pressure from his father and market forces suggests the lack of power that apprentices had in relation to their masters.

I WENT TO MARKET with my father every day, at length I found for myself a master by the name of John Paxton [a shoemaker], a resident in Water street in the city of New York, to him I went upon probation of a fortnight's duration, and staid with him a

Excerpt from William Otter, Sr., *History of My Own Times: Or the Life and Adventures of William Otter, Sr., Comprising a Series of Events, and Musical Incidents.* Altogether original excerpted in *Keepers of the Revolution*, Paul A. Gilje and Howard B. Rock, eds. (Ithaca: Cornell University Press, 1992), 46–48.

week all but three days, and then put out. From there I went home again, my father asked me how I liked the trade; to that enquiry I answered, that I did not like it at all, I had quit it; he asked me if I had told Mr. Paxton so; I told him I had; he asked me why I had quit; I told Mr. Paxton that it hurt me across my breast; my father asked me what are you going to learn now, I told him I did not know yet; I then walked about the city for two or three days.

I hunted for myself a master, in the meantime, and took a notion to learn the venetian blind making business, and found for myself a master in a man of the name of William Howard, who followed that business in Broadway, opposite the *park* he also took me on probation (as I had no notion to run a head of the wind) for two weeks; which is the established rule in the city, as to taking apprentices on probation. Mr. Howard put me at painting blinds; in that office I held out five days and found that the effects of the paints on my part was intolerable; I told Mr. Howard I believed I would leave him, that I could not stand it, I would go home; he said, well you must know best yourself, I do not intend to persuade you against your own will,—and there, and in manner aforesaid, ended my second apprenticeship, and I put out home. When I came home my father was absent, my mother asked me how I liked my new trade; I told her I had quit; why, said she, William you learn your trades quick; I told her yes; and what are you going to do now, continued my mother; I told her I did not know. In the evening my father came home; my mother told him that I had learned another trade; he then asked me had I quit again; I told him yes; he asked me if I had told Mr. Howard, that I intended to quit; I told him I had; he then said that was right. He then asked me what I would join next, I told him I thought I would try to learn the carpenter business; well, said he, seek for yourself another master, I told him I would; accordingly I went in quest of a master and got one, by the name of Gausman, a Scotchman, in Broadway: he put me to sawing out boards all that week; on Sunday I went home; father asked how I come on, I told him very well, he said he was glad to hear it, hoping I would get myself bound the next week, I told him I would wait till next week was over before I got myself bound; I kept on sawing boards until Thursday; I told the foreman I believed I would quit it, that I had the back-ache and the work was too hard: and without any further ceremony I put out for home, and so ended my third apprenticeship. My father asked me how I came on at the carpenter's business; I told him I had quit it, he then gave me to understand that he entertained the thought that hard work and myself had had a falling out; I told him yes, that I did not like it much. He told me in good earnest to make up my mind and go to some trade and stick to it and learn it, as I was fooling away my time to no purpose, in the way I had been leaving trades; as bye the bye, I was master of none; and that after a while my name would become so notorious that I could not get a master, as he wished to see me do well; and if I got a master again to get myself bound straightway. If I did not do that, I would never get a trade.

I then took a notion to team the bricklaying and plastering business, and went to hunt a master in good earnest, and found one by the name of Kenneth King. I asked him if he would take a boy and seam him his trade; he asked if I was the boy, I told him yes, he then asked me my name and where I lived, which inquiries I answered; he told me to bring my father there the next day, I told him I would; the next day about two o'clock according to promise my father and myself called to see Mr. King. My father signified a wish to have me bound instanter as I had so many masters, and flew as often too; Mr. King told my father he had no apprehension about him; but that he could make a good boy out of me, as he had no less than eight boys at that time; my father told him if it suited, he would like to have me bound on the spot, to which Mr. King said he had no objections if I was agreed; I told him I was perfectly satisfied, and we went straight to a squire-shop [lawyer's office] and got myself bound for four years. The next morning I went to work in my new birth [berth], and worked on till Saturday evening; I asked permission of my master to go home and see my parents, he consented I might go provided I returned on Sunday evening; I told him I would; I went home, and father asked me how I come on, I told him very well; he asked if I liked my trade and my master, I told him I did; he said he was very glad to hear it, hoped that I would stay and team my trade and make myself master of it. My mother said that she was glad that I had found a man and trade that I liked.

QUESTIONS

1. Was William Otter lazy, or would any reasonable person have resisted the kinds of work Otter was doing as an apprentice?
2. Was Otter lucky to have gotten any job?
3. Why would any master take a chance on an apprentice he did not know?

William Manning's Plan for a "Labouring Society," 1798

The early national period of the United States was a time of great intellectual ferment. Across the new nation, Americans of varied backgrounds grappled with the difficulties of putting the principles of the Declaration of Independence and the Constitution into practice. Among other questions, Americans wondered how people with little formal education and few personal connections to their leaders could understand the complex politics of the era.

Enter William Manning (1747–1814), a Massachusetts farmer and Jeffersonian Republican. In his manifesto, The Key of Libberty: Shewing the Causes why a Free Government Has Always Failed, and a Remidy Against It, *Manning posits that educated, professional men have their societies to help them understand a complex world, so workers and farmers should have the same. Despite very little formal schooling, Manning's ideas about an ideal "Labouring Society" would be reiterated in broad-based labor movements for centuries to come.*

BUT SOME MAY think that [forming a Labouring Society and publishing a magazine for workers on current events] will be a slow way to bring about a Reformation in our Circumstances. But if a large majority of the peopel are Republicans (which I dout not), ondly let them do as the roiallest do, vote no person into any office (even not in the towns) but what they are confident are true Republicans & purge the State legislatures from all fee offic-

Excerpt from William Manning, *The Key of Libberty: Shewing the Causes Why a Free Government Has Always Failed, and a Remidy Against It* (reprint) (Billerica, Mass.; The Manning Association, 1922), 65–67. All spelling and punctuation appears as it does in the original.

ers. Also play close attention to the choice of jurymen & make a common cause of detecting male administration & breaches of law by the Juditial & Executive officers (all which might be easily done if such a society was formed), it would soone make an ods in all the Departments of Government. They would all feel as acting in the presents of their Constituants & act as servents & not masters. Also by being thus furnished with the meens of knowledge, all impositions of all ordirs of men might be detectted & surpressed, & all hurtful fashions & customes Might be reformed, and Agruculture, Manifactoryes, Industries & Econimy promoted. For it is for the want of such meens of information that a grate parte of the studdyes & improvements of larnt men & Societyes established for these purposes are intirely lost.

If such a society was established our Representitives in Congress would have some reason to boste of our being the most free and inlightened peopel in the world, & it would in their present disputes incorage one side & depress the other as much as the memorials & petitions did that ware sent their in favour of the Brittish treety.

Such a Society would convince the world that Emarica can & will be free, & would do more to prevent a war with France than all we have in our power to do other ways.

And I have often had it impressed on my mind that in some way as this Society might be organised throughout the world as well as government, & by sotial corraspondance & mutual consestions all differences might be settled, so that wars might be banished from the Earth. For it is from the pride & ambition of rulers & the ignorance of the peopel that wars arise, & no nation as a nation ever got anithing by making war on others, for what evr their conquests may have bin the plunder goes to a few individuals, & always increases the misiryes of more than it helpes.

For the prinsapel hapiness of a Man in this world is to eat & drink & injoy the good of his Labour, & to feal that his Life Libberty & property is secure, & not in the abundance he poseses nor in being the instrument of other mens miseryes. All the advantage of national dealings is commerce & the exchenge of the produce of one cuntry for another, which if it might be carried on without wars would increase the hapiness of all Nations. But as it is in general conducted it ads to the miseryes of mankind.

Thus my frinds I have tryed to describe to you (not in the language & stile of the Larned for I am not able) But in as plane a manner as I am capable, the Causes that have always destroyed free governments, & the daingerous circumstances we are brought into by said Causes. Also described what I think would prove a Remidy, which is not a costly one, for if it should once become general, confident I am that each penny laid out in it would save some pounds. I have also placed a Constitution at the close of this adress with a Covenant ready for signing, which though an imperfect one may answer for the beginning of said Society. And unless you see more difficulty in applying the Reamidy or less need of it than I do, you will immediately put it on foot & neaver give over untill such a Society is established on such a strong & lasting foundation that the gates of hell can never prevail against it—which may the Almighty grant is the sincear desire of

A LABOURER.

QUESTIONS

1. Manning sent this manifesto to the Jeffersonian paper in Boston, which refused to print it. Based on this excerpt, why do you think the editor made that decision?
2. Why does Manning believe that his organization will end wars?
3. What obstacles do you think a "Labouring Society" along the lines of Manning's would have faced in this era?

8

Recruiting Song of the Journeymen Cordwainers, ca. 1790

Songs have always been part of the tradition of worker organizing and protest. Singing was also part of the tradition of working-class saloon culture in the British Isles and northern Europe. Songs often expressed politically controversial views when authorities restricted access to printing presses.

In the earliest days of the new republic, workers banded together to safeguard wages and working conditions. The Federal Society of Journeymen Cordwainers, a shoemakers' union, existed from 1791 to 1806 and organized thirteen locals in the Philadelphia metropolitan area. In 1799, the union organized the first strike by a union that did not result in the union's dissolution immediately afterwards. This early strike was also the nation's first sympathy strike, as bootmakers (organized into a separate union) also walked out until the Journeymen Cordwainers' issues were settled.

Cordwainers! Arouse! The time has now come!
When our rights should be fully protected;
And every attempt to reduce any one
By all should be nobly rejected.

Fellow Craft-men! Arouse! We united should be
And each man should be hailed as a brother,
Organized we should be in this hallowed cause,
To love and relieve one another.

Excerpt from John McIlvaine, "Address to the Journeymen Cordwainers L. B. of Philadelphia," in Philip Foner, ed. *American Labor Songs of the Nineteenth Century* (Urbana: University of Illinois Press, 1975), 11.

Speak not of failure, in our attempt to maintain,
For our labor a fair compensation,
All that we want is assistance from you,
To have a permanent organization.

A commencement we've made, associations we have.
From one to thirteen inclusive.
Come join them my friends, and be not afraid,
Of them being in the least delusive.

Go join No. 1, and in it you'll find,
Men of courage and firmness, devoting
Their time and their money, in fact all they have
Your interest and mine they're promoting.

And join No. 2, if you wish to maintain
For your labor a fair compensation,
You will find them at work for you and for me
Their success has far beat expectation.

If you join No. 3, you will find them aroused,
For much do they dread the oppression
They have been subject to in years gone by,
Go give them a friendly expression.

Join No. 4, defer not a day,
But go and with them unite,
Ah! give them assistance, for you they're at work,
And they'll ten times your trouble requite.

If you join No. 5, you'll find them awake,
Awake to the pledge they have taken:
Their hearts are all true, add yours to them too,
And by them you ne'er shall be forsaken.

Or join No. 6, if you wish to be
Raised from your present condition,
To rank with mechanics in wages and name,
And be able to keep that position.

Nos. 7, 8, and 9, if you with them join,
Your interest they have justly at heart,
Their motives you'll love, and with them you'll move.
And from them you ne'er will depart.

Come join No. 10, if you wish to find,
Men whose hearts beat with love and devotion.
For the organization, to which they belong,
Come assist them to keep it in motion.

Or cross o'er to Jersey, if you be not afraid,
Of its native disease called the chills,
You will find men united their wages to raise,
On pump springs, welts, turns and heels.

Then join us, my friend, and be not afraid,
That we will extort from our employers
Prices that will injure our fair city's trade,
Or frighten away from us buyers.

QUESTIONS

1. In what ways do you think singing this song might have helped the strike?
2. What does the last verse mean? What might have scared listeners to the union's message?
3. What is the significance of love and devotion in the lyrics of the song? Why did its author choose such romantic imagery?

9

Wendell Phillips Compares Northern Workers and Slaves, 1865

Wendell Phillips (1811–1884), a well-known Boston abolitionist, turned his attention to workers' issues after the Civil War abolished slavery. In this speech, sponsored by Boston's Daily Evening Voice *newspaper, Phillips states his support for the eight-hour day and reminds workers of their need to vote for candidates who will endorse it, no matter which party they represent.*

While it is logical to assume that workers would organize in order to improve their wages, a shorter workday was also an important demand during the late nineteenth century. The twelve-hour day and six-day week were common in many industries, especially those industries that depended on unskilled or immigrant labor. Nevertheless, the eight-hour day did not become the standard workday in the United States until after World War I.

THEREFORE I SAY it is a fair division of a man's day—eight hours for sleep, eight hours for work, eight hours for his soul. [Applause.] Eight hours for his own, to idle if he pleases, to rest, to study if he pleases—to improve himself. It is not my business to say—"Sir, you shall not have the leisure unless you come under bonds to use it well." It is no business of mine how he uses what belongs to him. I do not go to the millionaire on Beacon street and say to him—"Sir, the laws of Massachusetts will not protect your bank unless according to my ideas you use it well." He has a right to his bank stock, and to do with it, under God,

Excerpt from Wendell Phillips, "Remarks at the Mass Meeting of Workingmen in Faneuil Hall, Nov. 2, 1865." (Boston: Voice Printing and Publishing Company, 1865), 8–10.

what he pleases. I may argue with him, I shall, [laughter] I may agitate in order to induce him to do certain things with it. When you have eight hours leisure I shall be with a bayonet at your heels trying to drive you into useful and honorable use of it. Be sure of that. But my first object is to give it to you, since it belongs to you.

Again, in claiming this, fairly considered, our right, we are not infringing the rights of any man. No man's rights, properly considered, interfere with any other man's rights. Show me the rights of a man or a class, and I will show you something with which nobody else has a right to interfere. You know I have been told on this platform, for twenty years, that the negro did not deserve his freedom, and would idle it away. My reply was—"What God gave him he shall have, and he is responsible to God for using it well or ill." My view, therefore, of this reform, is simply this: It is an endeavor to discover the true relations between labor and capital, and arrange matters in accordance with it. It is an endeavor to give the laboring classes of Massachusetts more leisure, and give them therefore better opportunity to become more intelligent. I defy a million of men, having got leisure and comfort, not to improve. There is no such instance in history. It is the universal excuse and pretence of the oppressor that they will not. In 1789, the talk of the nobles of France was—"the peasant is naturally idle, and would not work if he could live without it." But France rose up and broke her chains, and although the throne there rests in theory on universal suffrage, all feudalism abolished, still Frenchmen set example to the world in their painstaking and patient industry. So in regard to the system of slavery at the South. Men said—"the negro will never work unless you whip him to it." But we've tried it, and find Mr. Cash is a more efficient master than Mr. Lash.

The cry here is—"You can't make a white laborer work unless you starve him." I don't believe it. The cry here is in the same spirit—"drag a man down to absolute necessity, hang his wife and children like dead weights to him; let him have no hope outside a factory, with its fourteen or eleven hours; then he'll work; you have starved him to it, and it is the only motive that the working man will obey." I don't believe it. At any rate I wish to lift the weight off a while, and see if it be true. No harm in the experiment. In other words, I want eight hours a day for work, and eight hours a day for leisure, secured as far as possible to the laboring masses of this nation. Give them the opportunity to show what they'll do with leisure. My plan has another element. Eight hours of leisure and public, free evening schools for adults, to teach them everything worth knowing. No one who was neglected in childhood shall have, in his poverty, any excuse for continuing an ignorant man. Leisure, Schools and Libraries—the means to use that leisure well—that is the programme.

QUESTIONS

1. How would you summarize Phillips' rationale for the eight-hour day?
2. To what extent do you think workers followed Phillips's advice about how to spend their eight hours of free time?
3. Should leisure time be considered a right?

10

"Address of the National Labor Union to the People of the United States," 1870

The end of the Civil War brought economic opportunities amid wide-spread national disorder. Before the war, most unions in America were local organizations. Only a few represented workers from more than one city. And few attempts to organize on a regional scale sur-vived beyond the next economic downturn.

Building on previous efforts that united workers from different trades, the National Labor Union formed in 1866. Although the National Labor Union was not a truly national organization like the later Knights of Labor or the American Federation of Labor, it set important precedents for organizing workers across trade boundaries.

In this pamphlet, generated by the NLU's executive board, the union is trying to make its case for an eight-hour day. Although the NLU would break up in the early 1870s, its eight-hour-day campaign would be taken up by other national unions.

LABOR AND ITS RIGHTS.

WE HOLD THESE TRUTHS to be self-evident: That the rights of all use-ful labor are unitary and can never conflict; that labor has a common cause and interest in all efforts to elevate and improve the condition of the toiling masses; that no class of laborers can be excluded from our efforts and sympathies without the grossest injustice. We, therefore invite to our co-operation all classes of laborers, male and female; for this is a struggle for liberty and

Excerpt from *Address of the National Labor Union to the People of the United States on Money, Land, and other Subjects of National Importance* (Washington, DC: McGill & Witherow, Printers and Stereotypers, 1870), 19–21.

justice for all useful labor. We tender to all such our sympathies, whether united to us by organic ties or not, and hail them as coworkers in a common cause. Gradually we are getting rid of the crudities inherent to a new movement; gradually the objectionable features are melting away, until we can see the hour fast approaching when the marshaled masses, without a jarring discord, shall move in solid phalanx upon the enemies—ignorance, poverty, vice, crime, as they rear their hydra heads through the institutions of the past.

HOURS OF LABOR.

This subject has already received considerable attention and some legislation; and we deem it but just that we should express our views, and give our reasons for those views.

We deem eight hours per day for labor, eight for eating, recreation, and culture, and eight for rest, the most natural and equitable division of time in our country. The power of men and animals is properly expressed by three quantities: force, velocity, and time. In every organization there is a fixed value of these quantities subject to use, beyond which we cannot go without injury. The best formula for the highest results from these quantities is the above division.

This division is in harmony with the Encyclopædia Brittanica, the recognized authority of all scientific men in measuring the forces of nature. One of the oldest and most philanthropic institutions makes this division: eight for the usual avocations of life, eight for the service of God and the relief of worthy brothers, and eight for refreshment and sleep. This division is based on scientific and natural laws, and is supported by Franklin, Combe on the Constitution of Man, Dick, and many medical men, all writers on physical health, as well as insurance actuaries. All these most unequivocally declare that all excessive labor diminishes power and hastens death. Dick alleges, and very justly, that the fatigue of excessive labor tends to induce intemperance, while the proper medium increases power and tends to virtue and longevity.

It will not be denied that ten or fourteen hours a day deprives the toiler of disposition, opportunity, and capacity to rise in the scale of moral and intellectual being; that it denies him all social and physical recreation, and makes him a mere beast of burden for his master, the capitalist. On the other hand, as the wages of labor rise and the hours of labor are shortened, the thinking, skillful worker finds time and means to improve his methods and develop useful inventions. Since these improved conditions there has been a vast increase in labor-saving inventions, and it only remains now to improve these conditions, that all labor, by whomsoever performed, shall have equal pay, and all inventors shall have the control of the products of their brains as well as muscles, and be no longer the slaves of the capitalist.

The Issue Made Up.

On the one side are arrayed the bankers, usurers, speculators, and all who live by preying on the producing classes through subtile fiscal contrivances and the usurpation of the public domain. On the other side are the enterprising wealth-producing classes, in all departments of useful labor, calling, or profession— in a word, all who earn a living by *honest industry.*

R. F. Trevellick, President
A. T. Cavis, First Vice President.
C. Kuhm, Second Vice President
Council { A. Campbell,
             A. M. Puett,
H. J. Walls, Secretary.

Questions

1. How and why do the authors of this broadside appeal to religious and scientific reasoning?
2. Who is included in the National Labor Union's definition of "workers?" Who is left out?
3. Do you think the authors of this piece make an effective case for organizing? Why or why not?

Working-Class Culture

Illustration of the "terrific and fatal" riot at the New York Astor Place Opera House, 1849. No. WHi-10305, courtesy Wisconsin Historical Society.

11

Anonymous Account of the Astor Place Riot, 1849

By the mid-nineteenth century, the industrial revolution had created a well-defined class structure in the major cities of Europe and the United States. Tensions between members of the working class and upper class could explode at any time, even against the incongruous background of Shakespearean theatre.

Edwin Forrest and William C. Macready were two of the best-known actors of their generation. Forrest, a Philadelphia native, was known as "The American Tragedian," as he was the first U.S.-born actor to perform internationally. Macready, though born in Ireland, was identified as the leading British interpreter of Shakespeare and other serious theatre.

The two men enjoyed a friendly rivalry until Forrest criticized Macready's interpretation of Hamlet *in an 1846 performance. From that point onward, the rivalry between the two men grew sharper.*

Back in the United States, elite, Anglophilic theatergoers supported Macready's performances. At the same time, working-class theatergoers, who resented Macready's anti-American comments, supported Forrest. Class-based hostility between fans of each actor culminated in the Astor Place riot on May 10, 1849, in which twenty-three people, many of them innocent bystanders, died after local militias fired on crowds demonstrating outside the theater. Observers immediately interpreted the riot and its suppression as symptomatic of broader class-based rivalries.

Excerpt from Anonymous, "Account of the Terrific and Fatal Riot at the New-York Astor Place Opera House, On the night of May 10, 1849." (New York: H. M. Ranney, 1849), 18, 19, 25–27, 31–32.

THE [NEW YORK CITY] MAYOR, Mr. Woodhull, advised [theater own-
ers] Niblo and Hackett to close the house, and to avoid a riot, and
the probabl[e] destruction of property and life; but these gentlemen were determined to stand upon their rights, and the city
authorities decided, after consulting together, to sustain them, if
necessary, with all the force at their disposal. Mr. Matsell, the
chief of police, was asked if the civil force at his disposal would
be sufficient for the preservation of the peace, and though he had
nine hundred salaried policemen at his disposal, and the power
of calling in specials at discretion, he gave it as his opinion that
this force was not sufficient. It was thought necessary to call out
the military.

It has been boldly questioned whether all these extraordinary preparations would have been made to protect the legal rights
of humble citizens. Rich and influential men had invited Mr.
Macready to play at the aristocratic Opera House. Suppose it had
been some third-rate actor at the Chatham; suppose the request
for him to play had come from the patrons of that establishment.
The abstract question of right would have been the same; but
there are many who would doubt whether the city authorities
would have taken the extraordinary measure of calling out the
military—and this was probably the first time such a thing was
ever done under any but the most despotic governments. [. . .]

It would seem, after the publication of the card, signed by
Washington Irving, Charles King, and about fifty others, denounc-
ing the outrages of Monday night [when a smaller riot in the Opera
House stopped Macready's performance], and pledging themselves to sustain Macready, that the contest took on a new character. Macready was a subordinate personage, and he was to be
put down less on his own account, than to spite his aristocratic
supporters. The question became not only a national, but a social one. It was the rich against the poor—the aristocracy against
the people; and this hatred of wealth and privilege is increasing
throughout the world, and ready to burst out whenever there is
the slightest occasion. The rich and well-bred are too apt to de-
spise the poor and ignorant, and they must not think it strange if
they are hated in return. [. . .]

The scene which followed the firing of the military, beggars
all description. The wounded, the dying, and the dead, were scat-

tered in every direction. There were groans of agony, cries for help, and oaths of vengeance. The dead and the wounded were borne to the drug stores at the corners of Eighth street and Broadway, and Third Avenue, and others in the vicinity, and surgeons were summoned to attend them. Some were conveyed by the police to the Fifteenth Ward Station House, and a few were carried to the City Hospital. Some of the dead and wounded were laid out upon the billiard tables of Vauxhall Saloon, a large crowd gathered around, and speeches were made by excited orators.

Had none but those actively engaged in the riots been shot by the military, these details would have been sufficiently melancholy. But even then, we are to consider that the men who composed the mob, may have acted, under ordinary circumstances, like honest and respectable citizens. A mob is composed of the same men in a state of temporary insanity, and they should be treated accordingly. Sober and quiet citizens, acting under such a temporary excitement, have committed the greatest outrages. They should be restrained, but not sacrificed, unless under the most imperative necessity.

The morning of the eleventh of May was one of sad excitement in the city of New York. The extent of the calamity, the number of the dead and wounded, made a deep and solemn impression. Public opinion was very much divided. The more excitable breathed threats of vengeanece, and the military were kept under arms during that and the following day. A meeting was called in the Park, of "Citizens opposed to the destruction of Human Life." Several thousands assembled, and resolutions were passed, thoroughly condemning the authorities for not exhausting the civil power before calling out the military, and characterizing the sacrifice of life as "the most wanton, unprovoked and murderous outrage ever perpetrated in the civilized world;" and calling upon the Grand Jury to indict the Mayor, Recorder and Sheriff, for ordering the military to fire on the citizens. Exciting and inflammatory speeches were made by Edward Strahan, Isaiah Rynders, and Mike Walsh, but the meeting separated without disturbance. [. . .]

A distinguished clergyman of the city, preaching on the subject of the riot, says of Macready and his right to act—"Though he had been the meanest of his kind, he should have been protected here to the conclusion of his announced engagement, if an army of ten thousand men had been required to to wait upon his movements, and a ship of war chartered to convey him to his native land. We have done something to vindicate order and law, and we ought to have done more."

A zeal for the rights of Mr. Macready and his friends, and for the cause of law and order is commendable—but it must not be forgotten that other rights must have been violated, or this riot could never have taken place. These ignorant men had a right to education, and to such conditions of cultivation, as would have made them intelligent men and good citizens. They would never have raised their hands against society, had society done its duty to them. Before they committed this wrong, they had been most deeply wronged themselves; and it would be better to provide ten thousand schoolmasters to instruct people, than ten thousand dollars to prevent the result of their ignorance.

Men can be zealous and indignant about the rights of play actors, or their patrons—and we have no disposition to deny their rights, or to interfere with the lawful exercise of them—but they forget in how many ways the rights of our brethren are violated, and not a word is said in their behalf. Give every man the natural and social rights that belong to him and we should have few crimes and outrages to complain of, and law and order could be maintained without standing armies or ships of war.

When we go deep into the investigation of social wrongs, we shall find that society brings upon itself the very evils it attempts to subdue. Society, by an unjust distribution of the avails of industry, enables a few men to become rich, and consigns a great mass to hopeless poverty, with all its deprivations and degradations. This poverty produces ignorance, the sense of injustice, grovelling tastes, and a loss of all high ambition. The only wonder is that under such circumstances of wrong and outrage, men are so forebearing, so honest, and so orderly. The only wonder is that more crimes are not committed against both property and life. Thousands of poor people know that they are robbed and plundered every day of their lives—they feel bitterly the hardships and injustice of their lot; but how calmly do they wait God's justice to set them right! How few of them comparatively attempt to right their own wrongs, and to sieze [sic] upon a portion of what society withholds from them!

This terrible tragedy is a lesson to us all. None can escape its warning. We are all responsible, all guilty; for we make a part of a society that has permitted thousands of its members to grow up in poverty and ignorance, and exposed to the temptations of vice and crime. This mob is but a symptom of our social condition, and it points out a disease to which we should lose no time in applying a proper remedy.

QUESTIONS

1. Where do the sympathies of the writer lie? How do you know?
2. How could a rivalry between two actors come to symbolize broad class conflicts in nineteenth-century New York City?
3. Are "we all responsible, all guilty" for the injustices of the society we live in, as the author suggests?

Samuel Gompers Describes
Cigar Rolling in His Autobiography

Samuel Gompers is best known as a founder and first president of the American Federation of Labor, the first permanent national federation of labor unions in the United States. He served in that post (with the exception of one year in the 1890s) from 1886 to his death in 1924.

Before achieving fame in this post, Gompers, an immigrant from England, worked as a cigarmaker. In this excerpt from his autobiography, Gompers discusses the relationship between the social bonds of cigarmakers and their militancy against management. The culture of cigarmakers developed out of their circumstances. Unlike other industrial workers, cigarmakers had the opportunity to bond because of the close proximity in which they labored, their shared specialized skill, and their relative ethnic homogeneity. This made it far easier for them to organize and strike than it was for other immigrant populations working in manufacturing jobs who often worked in large factories, had few skills, and perhaps could not even speak the language of their co-workers.

IN THOSE EARLY YEARS the fraternal or lodge movement absorbed practically all my leisure. It was its human side that drew me. I saw in it a chance for men to develop and to lend a helping hand when most needed. The lodge was to me a form of education extension. In time its limitations became evident, for I had been making ready to reach out for something bigger and more fundamental. I was a member of the union in my trade for practical

From *Seventy Years of Life and Labour,* by Samuel Gompers, © 1925 by Samuel Gompers, renewed © 1953 by Gertrude Gleaves Gompers. Used by permission of Dutton, a division of Penguin Group (USA) Inc.

reasons, while my idealism and sentiment found expression in fraternalism. As yet I did not understand that the philosophy and scope of the trade union movement could be made broad and deep enough to include all the aspirations and needs of the wage-earner.

I attended union meetings rather casually in the sixties. Local Cigarmakers' Union No. met in a room over the saloon of Garrett Berlyn, 46 East Broadway. He was the father of Barney Berlyn who was one of our members and was elected corresponding secretary in 1870. Barney afterwards became an ardent Socialist. Our union was not very strong. It was affiliated to the old National Union of Cigarmakers organized in 1864 and later to the Cigarmakers' International Union of America, as the movement was called after the reorganization in 1867, John J. Junio of Syracuse was president. At that time the cigarmakers of this country were as a rule Armenians, Englishmen, and Hollanders. There were a few Germans who had come to the United States from 1855 to 1867. After the Civil War, when cigarmaking began to develop from a house trade into a factory industry, the proportion of German workmen was largely increased.

There was a vast difference between those early unions and the unions of today. Then there was no law or order. A union was a more or less definite group of people employed in the same trade who might help each other out in special difficulties with the employer. There was no sustained effort to secure fair wages through collective bargaining. The employer fixed wages until he shoved them down to a point where human endurance revolted. Often the revolt started by an individual whose personal grievance was sore, who rose and declared: "I am going on strike. All who remain at work are scabs." Usually the workers went out with him.

I remember being busily at work one day when Conrad Kuhn, president of the Cigarmakers' Unions of New York City, entered the shop and announced: "This shop is on strike." Kuhn was a large, fine-looking man, with a stentorian voice that could be heard in every portion of the shop. Without hesitation we all laid down our work and walked out. That was the way it was done in the early days. We had no conception of constructive business tactics beginning with presentation of demands and negotiation to reach an agreement.

Whether we won or lost that strike I don't remember, but the union had no money at the end. Kuhn gave valiant service to us, but his family was actually suffering. It was after the big strike of 1872 that he had to leave the trade. The Turners helped him find a position where he could earn a living, for of course he was black-listed.

The union was generally in a precarious condition financially. Strike funds were never assured, and there were no other benefits. The union represented a feeling of community of burdens of those working in the same industry. It had to acquire a new meaning before it became an industrial agency. It had to strengthen its defensive resources and develop cohesive forces. But that was not only the embryonic stage of unionism; it was the fledgling period of industry. Industrial production was uncouth, unscientific, just about as planless as unionism. Management, accountancy, salesmanship, elimination of waste were in the rule-of-thumb stage. Factory architecture and industrial sanitation were undeveloped sciences.

Any kind of an old loft served as a cigar shop. If there were enough windows, we had sufficient light for our work; if not, it was apparently no concern of the management. There was an entirely different conception of sanitation both in the shop and in the home of those days from now. The toilet facilities were a water-closet and a sink for washing purposes, usually located by the closet. In most cigar shops our towels were the bagging that came around the bales of Havana and other high grades of tobacco. Cigar shops were always dusty from the tobacco stems and powdered leaves. Benches and work tables were not designed to enable the workmen to adjust bodies and arms comfortably to work surface. Each workman supplied his own cutting board of lignum vitae and knife blade.

The tobacco leaf was prepared by strippers who drew the leaves from the heavy stem and put them in pads of about fifty. The leaves had to be handled carefully to prevent tearing. The craftsmanship of the cigarmaker was shown in his ability to utilize wrappers to the best advantage to shave off the unusable to a hairbreadth, to roll so as to cover holes in the leaf and to use both hands so as to make a perfectly shaped and rolled product. These things a good cigarmaker learned to do more or less mechanically, which left us free to think, talk, listen, or sing. I loved the freedom of that work, for I had earned the mind-freedom that accompanied skill as a craftsman. I was eager to learn from discussion and reading or to pour out my feeling in song. Often we chose someone to read to us who was a particularly good reader, and in payment the rest of us gave him sufficient of our cigars so he was not the loser. The reading was always followed by discussion, so we learned to know each other pretty thoroughly. We learned who could take a joke in good spirit, who could marshal his thoughts in an orderly way, who could distinguish clever sophistry from sound reasoning. The fellowship that grew between congenial shopmates was something that lasted a lifetime.

QUESTIONS

1. How did the cigarmakers' shared culture contribute to their militancy?
2. What made the cigarmaker's job skilled work?
3. Considering the difficult circumstances that cigarmakers faced, why does Gompers look back on his days in this job with nostalgia?

Elizabeth Keckley Explains Why She Fought Back

The word "slave" conjures up images of a servant who must bend her will entirely to her master. In fact, slaves frequently controlled considerable resistance to the will of their masters, despite the threat of whippings or beatings. Sometimes this resistance came as a result of support from other slaves, but sometimes it was just a matter of personality.

Elizabeth Keckley was a North Carolina slave who would go on to become the personal dressmaker for Abraham Lincoln's wife, Mary. Her autobiography, Behind the Scenes, or, Thirty Years a Slave, and Four Years in the White House, *deals primarily with her White House years. In fact, it was so controversial that pressure from the Lincoln family led to its removal from the market. This selection from the beginning of the book deals with her resistance to a particularly cruel master. It is worth noting that Keckley was the only slave in this household.*

WHEN I WAS ABOUT fourteen years old I went to live with my master's eldest son, a Presbyterian minister. His salary was small, and he was burdened with a helpless wife, a girl that he had married in the humble walks of life. She was morbidly sensitive, and imagined that I regarded her with contemptuous feelings because she was of poor parentage. I was their only servant, and a gracious loan at that. They were not able to buy me, so my old master sought to render them assistance by allowing them the benefit of

Excerpt from Elizabeth Keckley, *Behind the Scenes, or, Thirty Years a Slave, and Four Years in the White House* (New York: G. W. Carleton and Co., 1868), 31–38.

my services. From the very first I did the work of three servants, and yet I was scolded and regarded with distrust. The years passed slowly, and I continued to serve them, and at the same time grew into strong, healthy womanhood. I was nearly eighteen when we removed from Virginia to Hillsboro', North Carolina, where young Mr. Burwell took charge of a church. The salary was small, and we still had to practise the closest economy. Mr. Bingham, a hard, cruel man, the village schoolmaster, was a member of my young master's church, and he was a frequent visitor to the parsonage. She whom I called mistress seemed to be desirous to wreak vengeance on me for something, and Bingham became her ready tool. During this time my master was unusually kind to me; he was naturally a good-hearted man, but was influenced by his wife. It was Saturday evening, and while I was bending over the bed, watching the baby that I had just hushed into slumber, Mr. Bingham came to the door and asked me to go with him to his study. Wondering what he meant by his strange request, I followed him, and when we had entered the study he closed the door, and in his blunt way remarked: "Lizzie, I am going to flog you." I was thunderstruck, and tried to think if I had been remiss in anything. I could not recollect of doing anything to deserve punishment, and with surprise exclaimed: "Whip me, Mr. Bingham! what for?"

"No matter," he replied, "I am going to whip you, so take down your dress this instant. "

Recollect, I was eighteen years of age, was a woman fully developed, and yet this man coolly bade me take down my dress. I drew myself up proudly, firmly, and said: "No, Mr. Bingham, I shall not take down my dress before you. Moreover, you shall not whip me unless you prove the stronger. Nobody has a right to whip me but my own master, and nobody shall do so if I can prevent it."

My words seemed to exasperate him. He seized a rope, caught me roughly, and tried to tie me. I resisted with all my strength, but he was the stronger of the two, and after a hard struggle succeeded in binding my hands and tearing my dress from my back. Then he picked up a rawhide, and began to ply it freely over my shoulders. With steady hand and practised eye he would raise the instrument of torture, nerve himself for a blow, and with fearful force the rawhide descended upon the quivering flesh. It cut the skin, raised great welts, and the warm blood trickled down my back. Oh God! I can feel the torture now—the terrible, excruciating agony of those moments. I did not scream; I was too proud to let my tormentor know what I was suffering. I closed my lips firmly, that not even a groan might escape from them, and I stood like a statue while the keen lash cut deep into my flesh. As soon as I was released, stunned with pain, bruised and bleeding, I went home and rushed into the presence of the pastor and his wife, wildly exclaiming: "Master Robert, why did you let Mr. Bingham flog me? What have I done that I should be so punished?"

"Go away," he gruffly answered, "do not bother me."

I would not be put off thus. "What *have* I done? I *will* know why I have been flogged. "

I saw his cheeks flush with anger, but I did not move. He rose to his feet, and on my refusing to go without an explanation, seized a chair, struck me, and felled me to the floor. I rose, bewildered, almost dead with pain, crept to my room, dressed my bruised arms and back as best I could, and then lay down, but not to sleep. No, I could not sleep, for I was suffering mental as well as bodily torture. My spirit rebelled against the unjustness that had been inflicted upon me, and though I tried to smother my anger and to forgive those who had been so cruel to me, it was impossible. The next morning I was more calm, and I believe that I could then have forgiven everything for the sake of one kind word. But the kind word was not proffered, and it may be possible that I grew somewhat wayward and sullen. Though I had faults, I know now, as I felt then, harshness was the poorest inducement for the correction of them. It seems that Mr. Bingham had pledged himself to Mrs. Burwell to subdue what he called my "stubborn pride." On Friday following the Saturday on which I was so savagely beaten, Mr. Bingham again directed me come to his study. I went, but with the determination to offer resistance should he attempt to flog me again. On entering the room I found him prepared with a new rope and a new cowhide. I told him that I was ready to die, but that he could not conquer me. In struggling with him I bit his finger severely, when he seized a

heavy stick and beat me with it in a shameful manner. Again I
went home sore and bleeding, but with pride as strong and defiant as ever. The following Thursday Mr. Bingham again tried to
conquer me, but in vain. We struggled, and he struck me many
savage blows. As I stood bleeding before him, nearly exhausted
with his efforts, he burst into tears, and declared that it would be
a sin to beat me any more. My suffering at last subdued his hard
heart; he asked my forgiveness, and afterwards was an altered
man. He was never known to strike one of his servants from that
day forward. Mr. Burwell, he who preached the love of Heaven,
who glorified the precepts and examples of Christ, who expounded
the Holy Scriptures Sabbath after Sabbath from the pulpit, when
Mr. Bingham refused to whip me any more, was urged by his
wife to punish me himself. One morning he went to the wood-
pile, took an oak broom, cut the handle off, and with this heavy
handle attempted to conquer me. I fought him, but he proved the
strongest. At the sight of my bleeding form, his wife fell upon her
knees and begged him to desist. My distress even touched her
cold, jealous heart. I was so badly bruised that I was unable to
leave my bed for five days. I will not dwell upon the bitter an-
guish of these hours, for even the thought of them now makes
me shudder. The Rev. Mr. Burwell was not yet satisfied. He re-
solved to make another attempt to subdue my proud, rebellious
spirit—made the attempt and again failed, when he told me, with
an air of penitence, that he should never strike me another blow;
and faithfully he kept his word. These revolting scenes created a
great sensation at the time, were the talk of the town and neighborhood, and I flatter myself that the actions of those who had
conspired against me were not viewed in a light to reflect much
credit upon them.

Questions

1. Why did Keckley resist being beaten even though this resistance led to more beatings?
2. Was allowing Keckley to be beaten good labor management from her master's point of view? Explain.
3. Does the fact that Keckley was the only slave in the household make her master's actions more or less understandable?

James Burn on Work, Community, and Mobility in Civil War America

Although many European visitors to the United States were initially fascinated with the nation's democratic government, they came to theorize about ways that democracy shaped broader trends in American culture.

Most observers were particularly interested in the contrast between the rigid class structure of Great Britain and the more fluid social structure in the United States, where people seemed to become rich overnight. James Dawson Burn (1802–1889), a British writer, spent three years in the United States during the Civil War. Although his work touched on the war's progress, he was mainly interested in home-front issues, especially American attitudes toward work. In this excerpt, Burn examines the pros and cons of Americans' economic and social mobility.

NOTHING CAN AFFORD a better proof of the scarcity of working men in the United States than the number of young men who keep flying from one business to another, few of whom ever serve any apprenticeship. By this means large numbers of men beyond the age of maturity are enabled to become masters of trades, who, had they remained in the old country, could never have had such opportunities of bettering their social condition. It may be inferred from this that, unlike the old country with its trade guilds, all branches of business are free and open. Human liberty, however, is only a comparative term. Although this is the land of liberty *par excellence*, there are many occasions when men are

Excerpt from James Dawson Burn, *Three Years Among the Working Classes in the United States During the War* (London: Smith, Elder and Co., 1865), 22–26.

not allowed to sell their labour to their own advantage without the certain prospect of a visit from some of the members of the Lynch family. The battle of labour and capital is frequently being fought here between associated bodies of men and their employers with all the acrimony and ill-feeling which selfishness and blind passion dictate. It is but a short time since the labourers employed at the docks in New York turned upon a number of coloured men and maltreated them in a most cruel manner because they presumed to sell their labour in the same market. It would seem to me one of the first principles of social liberty that men should possess the right to dispose of their labour in any way by which they might better their condition; but with the working men as with the strong in all other grades of society might is right where self-interest sits in judgment.

. . .

There is one circumstance in the condition of a stranger in this country which ought not to be lost sight of—and that is, the isolation in which he is almost sure to find himself. Men here form so many atoms in a mass, in which all individuality (with few exceptions) is swallowed up. The social machine is a great working power deriving little or no impulse from kindly feeling. That human sympathy which is ever a balm to grief, and which seldom fails to soothe men's minds in sorrow or misfortune, may exist, but as far as my observation goes, it is rarely either felt or seen among the working classes in America. I have conversed with men who have been in the country for several years, and who avowed that they never knew what it was to have a friend in the proper acceptation of the term, since they landed. Men may work together for months or years, and when they part and meet again they will "How d' do?" each other; but with this their interest in each other ends. While I am writing I have been nearly three years in the country, and during that time have never associated with a single being (if I leave my shopmates out of the question during hours of labour) beyond my own family. Nor from what I have observed of the people, do I see how it could be otherwise. The home feelings which conduce to the happiness of private families, and the kindness of disposition which they beget, are, [. . .] by no means common in America. If the members of private families are without affection for each other, it is not likely that friendship can form a bond of union in a community so reared.

One of the worst features in the character of the working classes is their savage dogmatism while discussing even ordinary subjects. There are three topics which form the stock in trade of both men and women in the workshops. These are country, religion, and politics. Many a little storm of passion is raised by these simple nouns; and though their discussion leads to angry and uncharitable feeling the battle never ceases.

In the course of a conversation I had with a fellow tradesman, a German, I asked him if he could not live as comfortably by his labour at home as he could in America?

"Yah," he replied, "ven I vas at hom I had more closh un more pleasures den I have here; in dis contrie is all de while going round for vork, in my contrie 'tish diffrents—ve stay all the whiles in one place."

"Why did you leave?"

"I no like to be the soger, so leaves un travels on de Continent."

"Did you work at your own trade in many of the European towns?"

"Yah; I vorked in Bremen, un Strausborgh, un Hamborgh in Shermany. I vorked in Varshaw in Poland, in Bucharest, Walachia, un in Smyrna; den I go to California, and stay dare tree year."

"You were at the gold digging there?"

"Yah!"

"Did you make any money while in California?"

"I makes seven hondred dollars, den I coms here an loss it all."

I have met with several Germans in my own business who had travelled over a great part of Europe; some of them had been in Australia, all had found their way to California, and, after varied fortunes, landed in the United States. My friend above was a Prussian German. I inquired if the Prussians enjoyed social and political liberty to anything like the same extent that the people in America did? He said that the people held the franchise by a property qualification; that men could follow any business they thought proper, and move from one place to another when it suited them.

QUESTIONS

1. In what ways do the emotional distance and personal freedom that Burn sees relate to each other?
2. How does the German worker support or complicate Burn's beliefs about lives of American workers?
3. Why does Burn record the German worker's answers in dialect, and what impact does the dialect have on you as you read it?

Part II: 1877–1914

AFTER 1877, THE PACE of industrialization in the United States accelerated rapidly. The application of new technologies led to the development of new goods such as structural steel for building skyscrapers. And in general these changes made it easier to produce better-quality goods at lower prices. Perhaps the best example of this is ready-to-wear clothing that customers could don without going to a tailor. Superior production techniques also led to surpluses of goods of all kinds. For example, the automatic cigarette rolling machine, developed in 1885, could produce 120,000 cigarettes in a day. Mass marketing and improvements in transportation made it easier to sell these goods all across the country.

In order to cope with their increasingly difficult circumstances, many families began to send women and children into the workforce (see number 16, Spargo). Since these workers were generally supported by a male breadwinner, employers knew they would work for less. After the turn of the century, both these trends accelerated. As with competition from immigrants, competition from women and children made the situation for native-born male workers even more difficult by driving down their wages. At the same time, long hours and an oversupply of laborers meant that the jobs all workers took became increasingly unsafe (see number 17, Potter).

Some workers, particularly those with few skills, had to accept these increasingly difficult terms and conditions of employment in order to survive. Other workers began to organize. The National Labor Union, which had formed in the years immediately following the Civil War, was the first nationwide cross-industry labor organization in American history. Starting in the late 1870s, a new national union emerged. The Knights of Labor organized most workers (even managers) because it believed that labor deserved greater reward for its sacrifice (see number 19, "Initiation Ceremony"). In 1886, Samuel Gompers and other trade union leaders organized the American Federation of Labor (AFL). A federation of craft unions, it became an important voice for workers on issues like changes in labor law and immigration restriction (see number 21, "Junius").

Increasingly, workers fought back against the changes that defined working life during this era by walking off the job. Sometimes they had the benefit of a trade union to help them, sometimes they did not. The first national strike in American history, the Great Railroad Strike of 1877, occurred at the beginning of this period. That strike, which paralyzed the nation's railroad system for weeks, would be followed by other disruptions in many industries. By the 1880s, the strike problem got so bad that people began to talk about "The Labor Question": how to get workers to accept the difficult terms and conditions of employment that industrialization created (see number 15, Darrow). Andrew Carnegie, the great steel magnate, thought he had found a solution to this problem by recognizing unions of skilled workers, but that temporary labor peace broke down in the Homestead Lockout of 1892. One of the most violent incidents of its day, this dispute was marked by a gun battle between strikers and armed guards hired by Carnegie's firm (see number 20, "Homestead Riots"). Another particularly violent incident in the history of American labor confrontations occurred in southern Colorado in 1914, when the state militia attacked a camp of striking miners' families with machine guns (see number 22, Jolly). Efforts by unionized mechanics to resist changes in production at the United States Government's Watertown, Massachusetts, arsenal in 1911 (see number 18, Cheney) suggest that even skilled workers faced great difficulty in controlling their workplace during this era.

Without aid from other workers, male workers sought control over other areas of their lives so that they could find some gratification. One outlet for on-the-job frustration was commercial sex, even if this meant exploiting female workers who faced economic circumstances more difficult than their own (see number 23, "Working Life of Prostitutes"). Another source of satisfaction was religion, which inspired a great deal of outrage from labor radicals for distracting workers from their exploitation (see number 26, Hill). The new mass culture of the early twentieth century also made workers' lives brighter (see number 27, McClean). At first, theater, films, and records catered to individual ethnic groups. Later on mass media appealed to Americans across ethnic divisions. But perhaps the most important source of satisfaction in workers' lives was their family and home life (see number 24, Byington). The quality of the menu on the steelworkers' tables is one of many explanations why the difficult circumstances of industrialization did not lead to fundamental changes in the organization of the American economy (see number 25, Sombart).

World War I marked the beginning of the end of accelerated industrialization in the United States. However, it also marked the beginning of significant government involvement in the ongoing struggle between employers and employees. That involvement would do much to define American life in the next three decades.

Work and Labor/ Management Relations

Breaker Boys, employed to separate coal from other rock, were common in mines throughout the country around the turn of the twentieth century. Courtesy Library of Congress, neg. #1806.

15

Clarence Darrow Considers the Labor Question, 1898

When people of the late-nineteenth and early-twentieth centuries discussed "The Labor Question," they were debating the best way to convince working people to accept the harsh conditions created by industrialization. Politicians, businesspeople, journalists—almost everyone in American society—considered how to address the concerns of an increasingly restless working class. More often than not, American employers looked to tighten control over employees rather than to change the harsh conditions they faced.

When the Woodworkers International Union organized a strike against the Paine Lumber Company of Oshkosh, Wisconsin, Company President George M. Paine turned to state authorities for help. Under Wisconsin law, they charged the General Secretary of the National Union, Thomas I. Kidd, and two local workers, with conducting a "criminal conspiracy" to hurt Paine's business. Kidd and his codefendants turned to the famed criminal defense attorney Clarence Darrow for help. Darrow, who had made his reputation defending American Railway Union President Eugene V. Debs after the infamous Pullman Strike of 1894, turned the case into an indictment of the excesses of the American capitalist system. In his summary for the jury, excerpted below, Darrow tried to create sympathy for the defendants by explaining the difficult circumstances that led working people to join unions. The tactic worked. Paine and his codefendants were acquitted.

Excerpt from Clarence Darrow, "Argument of Clarence S. Darrow in the case of the *State of Wisconsin* vs. *Thos. I. Kidd* . . . " (Chicago: Campbell Printers, 1900), 21–24.

NOW, GENTLEMEN, I want to say a few words in relation to the labor question, which is really the controversy involved in this case, because that is all there is of it. Back of all this prosecution is the effort on the part of George M. Paine to wipe these labor organizations out of existence, and you know it. That's all there is of it.

In many well-ordered penitentiaries outside of Oshkosh they have a rule that people cannot converse at all, and the reason is that they may not conspire. And down in the dark coal mines in the anthracite regions of Pennsylvania where those human moles burrow in the earth for the benefit of the great, monstrous greedy corporations that are corrupting the life-blood of the nation, there they work men in chain gangs, and put an Italian, an Austrian, a German, an American and a Bohemian together so they cannot understand each other when they speak, so that they may not combine and conspire, because in combination and in combination alone, is strength. They do this, gentlemen of the jury, so that each one of those tiny atoms, each poor laborer, with his little family, perhaps, around him, working for a dollar a day, or eighty cents a day, is bound to compete with the combination of men, with all the wealth that all their lives can create. On the one hand these powerful interests are organized thoroughly, completely, and they act together; and they turn to those poor slaves, whose liberty they take, and say to them, "We will consult with you, but come alone to our office, and then we will talk." They say this because they wish to meet the weak and puny and helpless single individual with the great and powerful wealth and strength of their mighty corporations. And that is what Paine said. "I would not answer the letter because it came from a labor organization, and I did not know who it was. I will meet my men alone and talk with them. There are only two parties to a contract, the employer and the employed." Yes, gentlemen, they would meet their men alone. Fie on you for hypocrites and cowards, who would combine every manufacturer in the city of Oshkosh, not into a "union," but into an "association." A body of employers living from the unpaid labor of the poor is an "association." A body of their slaves is a "labor union." George M. Paine says, "I will not meet your union; I will not meet your committee. If one of you has anything to say, come to me alone and talk." And they did go alone, and what did they get? Gentlemen, what did they get?

This was the beginning of the strike. It was not the speech of Thomas I. Kidd. All the orators on earth could never bring dissatisfaction and riot where justice rules; and all the hired lawyers on earth can never keep down the seething, boiling sea of discontent that is based on sin, and crime, and wrong. . . .

There was another man who worked in Paine's mill and he said, "I want a raise"; and the boss answered, "Well, you get out of here or I'll give you a raise in the pants." What beautiful gentlemen these are! Won't it be a pleasure, gentlemen of the jury, just to accommodate them by passing out a verdict of Guilty? This is the way they want to be met, singly and alone. After these men have toiled all these years and are growing old in their business and their service, they are kicked aside like dogs. Mark this, gentlemen, no one has disputed the statements, or any others; and they could not dispute them; they are absolutely true. This is the way the laboring men of Oshkosh were treated by the employers who had waxed great and rich at their expense. And you are asked to cure this discontent by sending Kidd to jail. Gentlemen, let me ask you, do you suppose that while George M. Paine pays a dollar and quarter a day for skilled labor, that there are jails enough on earth to hold the criminals who will rise in rebellion against such conditions? Aye, gentlemen, if the jails could have put down insurrection and rebellion, then you and I would not be living in America today. If the jails and the penitentiaries and the scaffolds could have strangled and wiped out rebellion and riot and insurrection, there would have been no America republic for us to protect and uphold. You gentlemen who wish to bring back the good old days of the past, you gentlemen with all your power and your wealth, cannot crush discontent and unrest from the hearts of men.

QUESTIONS

1. Why did Darrow want to make the case about Paine rather than the actions of the Woodworkers Union?
2. Was Darrow right about the revolutionary potential of the American working class?
3. Why do you think that George Paine believed that destroying the union was the best way to produce labor peace at his company?

16
John Spargo Examines Child Labor in the Glassmaking Industry, 1906

In the days before universal education, many children entered the paid labor force at a very young age. In the United States, where wage labor was rare before the 1820s, this phenomenon is commonly associated with the onset of industrialization. At first children worked because demand for labor was so high. During the late years of industrialization, most children who worked did so in order to make up for the deficiencies in the salaries of their parents.

By the turn of the twentieth century, Progressive reformers began to shine a spotlight on the nature of children's employment—as one of the excesses of industrial capitalism—in order to get this practice banned through state or federal legislation. Although children working in southern textile mills and coal mines attracted the most attention, children worked in many branches of American industry until the Fair Labor Standards Act finally banned this kind of labor nationwide in 1938. Here, the journalist John Spargo describes work for boys in glass factories at the turn of the twentieth century.

OF THE FIFTEEN DIVISIONS of the manufacturing industries, the glass factories rank next to the textile factories in the number of children they employ. In the year 1900, according to the census returns, the average number of workers employed in glass manufacture was 52,818, of which number 3529, or 6.88 per cent, were women, and 7116, or 13.45 per cent, were children under sixteen years of age. It will be noticed that the percentage of children employed is about the same as in the textile trades. There are

Excerpt from John Spargo, *The Bitter Cry of Children* (New York: Grosset & Dunlap, 1906), 154–61.

glass factories in many states, but the bulk of the industry is centred in Pennsylvania, Indiana, New Jersey, and Ohio. The total value of the products of the glass industry in the United States in 1900 was $56,539,712, of which amount the four states named contributed $46,209,918, or 82.91 per cent of the entire value. After careful investigation in a majority of the places where glass is manufactured in these four states, I am confident that the number of children employed is much larger than the census figures indicate. . . .

I shall never forget my first visit to a glass factory at night: It was a big wooden structure, so loosely built that it afforded little protection from draughts, surrounded by a high fence with several rows of barbed wire stretched across the top. I went with the foreman of the factory and he explained to me the reason for the stockade-like fence. "It keeps the young imps inside once we've got 'em for the night shift," he said. The "young imps" were, of course, the boys employed, about forty in number, at least ten of whom were less than twelve years of age. It was a cheap bottle factory, and the proportion of boys to men was larger than, is usual in the higher grades of manufacture. Cheapness and child labor go together,—the cheaper the grade of manufacture, as a rule, the cheaper the labor employed. The hours of labor for the "night shift" were from 5:30 P.M. to 3:30 A.M. I stayed and watched the boys at their work for several hours, and when their tasks were done saw them disappear into the darkness and storm of the night. That night, for the first time, I realized the tragic significance of cheap bottles. . . .

In the middle of the room was a large round furnace with a number of small doors, three or four feet from the ground, forming a sort of belt around the furnace. In front of these doors the glassblowers were working. With long wrought-iron blowpipes the blowers deftly took from the furnace little wads of waxlike molten "metal" which they blew into balls and then rolled on their rolling boards. These elongated rolls they dropped into moulds and then blew again, harder than before, to force the half-shaped mass into its proper form. With a sharp, clicking sound they broke their pipes away and repeated the whole process. There was not, of course, the fascination about their work that the more artistic forms of glass-blowing possess. There was none of that twirling of the blowpipes till they looked like so many magic wands which for centuries has made the glass-blower's art a delightful, half-mysterious thing to watch. But it was still wonderful to see the exactness of each man's "dip," and the deftness with which they manipulated the balls before casting them into the moulds.

Then began the work of the boys. By the side of each mould sat a "take-out boy," who, with tongs, took the half-finished bottles—not yet provided with necks—out of the moulds. Then other boys, called "snapper-ups," took these bodies of bottles in their tongs and put the small ends into gas-heated moulds till they were red hot. Then the boys took them out with almost incredible quickness and passed them to other men, "finishers," who shaped the necks of the bottles into their final form. Then the "carrying-in boys," sometimes called "carrier pigeons," took the red-hot bottles from, the benches; three or four at a time, upon big asbestos shovels to the annealing oven, where they are gradually cooled off to insure even contraction and to prevent breaking in consequence of too rapid cooling. The work of these "carrying-in boys," several of whom were less than twelve years old, was by far the hardest of all. They were kept on a slow run all the time from the benches to the annealing oven and back again. I can readily believe what many manufacturers assert, that it is difficult to get men to do this work, because men cannot stand the pace and get tired too quickly. It is a fact; however, that in many factories men are employed to do this work, especially at night. In other, more up-to-date factories it is done by automatic machinery. I did not measure the distance from the benches to the annealing oven, nor did I count the number of trips made by the boys; but my friend, Mr. Owen R. Lovejoy, has done so in a typical factory and very kindly furnished me with the results of his calculation. The distance to the annealing oven in the factory in question was one hundred feet, and the boys made seventy-two trips per hour, making the distance travelled in eight hours nearly twenty-two miles. Over half of this distance the boys were carrying their hot loads to the oven: The pay of these boys varies from sixty cents to a dollar for eight hours' work. About a year ago I gathered particulars of the pay of 257 boys in New Jersey and Pennsylvania; the lowest pay was forty cents per night and the highest a dollar and ten cents; while the average was seventy-two cents. . . .

The effects of the employment of young boys in glass factories; especially by night, are injurious from every possible point of view. The constant facing of the glare of the furnaces and the red-hot bottles causes serious injury to the sight. Minor accidents from burning are common. "Severe burns and the loss of sight are regular risks of the trade in glass-bottle making," says Mrs. Florence Kelley. Even more serious than the accidents are those physical disorders induced by the conditions of employment. Boys who work at night do not as a rule get sufficient or satisfactory rest by day. Very often they cannot sleep because of the noises made by younger children in and around the house; more often, perhaps, they prefer to play rather than to sleep. Indeed, most boys seem to prefer night work, for the reason that it gives them the chance to play during the daytime. Even where the mothers are careful and solicitous, they find it practically impossible to control boys who are wage-earners and feel themselves to be independent. This lack of proper rest, added to the heat and strain of their work, produces nervous dyspepsia. From working in draughty sheds where they are often, as one boy said to me in Zanesville, O., "burning on the side against the furnace and pretty near freezing on the other," they are frequently subject to rheumatism. Going from the heated factories to their homes, often a mile or so distant, perspiring and improperly clad, with their vitality at its lowest ebb, they fall ready victims to pneumonia and to its heir, the Great White Plague. In almost every instance when I have asked local physicians for their experience, they have named these as the commonest physical results. Of the fearful moral consequences there can be no question. The glass-blowers themselves realize this and, even more than the physical deterioration, it prevents them from taking their own children into the glass houses. One practically never finds the son of a glass-blower employed as a "sapper-up," or "carrying-in boy," unless the father is dead or incapacitated by reason of sickness. "I'd sooner see my boy dead than working here. You might as well give a boy to the devil at once as send him to a glass factory," said one blower to me in Glassborough, N.J.; and that is the spirit in which most of the men regard the matter.

QUESTIONS

1. Why would a boy be willing to work under the difficult circumstances that Spargo describes?
2. Should families have a right to send their children to work if they want?
3. Why might glass producers prefer hiring children to hiring adults?

Grace Potter Reports on Industrial Accidents in Niagara Falls, New York, 1913

During the the nineteenth century, the American legal system held that employees bore the responsibility for the effect of all risks to life and limb when they agreed to work for any employer. Shortly after the turn of the twentieth century, this began to change. Particularly after the infamous Triangle Shirtwaist Fire of 1911 (a New York City factory blaze which killed 146 nonunionized workers, almost all of whom were immigrant girls), state legislatures, and to a lesser extent the federal government, began to pass laws to protect the health and well-being of workers they felt were at risk.

The New York State Legislature created the Factory Investigating Commission after the Triangle fire to look at health and safety issues for workers in a wide range of industries. Here, Grace Potter, an investigator for the commission, reports information she collected about accidents from anonymous companies around the Niagara Falls area. The following four examples from the forty accidents Potter summarized are sufficient to demonstrate the risks to skilled and unskilled factory workers alike. Although the New York investigation led to a smattering of legislation, including workmen's compensation programs, the federal government did not become involved in regulating workplace safety until the creation of the Occupational Safety and Health Administration in 1970.

Excerpt from Grace Potter, "Forty Accidents Occurring in Plants at Niagara Falls," *Second Report of the Factory Investigating Committee*, 1913, Volume II: Appendices to Report (Albany: J. B. Lyon Company, Printers, 1913), 559–82.

1.

Accident: Inhaling chlorine gas; fatal.

Name: O. H——.

Nationality: American.

Age: Forty-one.

Married or single: Married. Three Children.

Date of Accident: January 22, 1911.

Establishment: Plant B.

Specific Work: Carrier for the chlorine chamber.

Date of Investigation: July 25, 1912.

Medical attention: Dr. E. G——.

Statement of case: Escaping chlorine gas was inhaled and caused unconsciousness. O. H. was found unconscious at five o'clock in the afternoon; he was taken out and laid in the snow, and as that did not revive him ether was given to counteract the effects of the chlorine gas. Then the man was walked home in the severe cold in the hope that he would recover both from chlorine gas and ether. No doctor was called by the company to attend him when overcome with gas nor help him recover from the effects of the ether. The family called a physician after the man was brought home. He died from bronchial pneumonia a week after he had inhaled from the gas.

Statement of wife: " . . . I wanted to know why they did not bring him home in a carriage or telephone me to send a carriage. They said they were afraid to let him ride, they must keep him active. It was 10:30 o'clock at night when they got him home. We called a doctor for him and four days after he came home he was a maniac. It required three men to hold him in his delirium. The doctor advised that intravenous injections of saline solutions be given after taking his blood out. When the blood was pumped out the odor of chlorine gas in it was distinct; the trained nurse pointed this out to me. The Sunday after he inhaled the gas he died. The company sent no word of any kind to me, and after waiting to hear from them I wrote asking what they were going to do. They settled October 14th through my lawyer, granting me $500. I am now nursing to support myself and three children."

Statement of Physician: "I attended this man in the illness which resulted in his death. It is true that his sickness was caused by the accident at the factory and the treatment which followed it before a physician was called."

11.
Accident: Injured by machinery; fatal.
Name: I. R——.
Nationality: Canadian.
Age: Forty-six.
Married or single: Married. Two children.
Date of accident: March 21, 1912.
Establishment: Plant F.
Work: Millwright.
Date of Investigation: July 31, 1912.
Medical Attention: Dr. H. A——.

Statement of case: While I. R—— was in the mill room repairing a shaft at Plant F, his clothes were caught in a sprocket on a line shaft. He was whirled about the shaft and badly mangled, both legs and one arm being broken. He was taken to the E—— Hospital, where he died March 24, 1912, of the shock following the accident.

Statement of fellow-workman: "He was caught in a screw which was projecting, when it should have been set in or protected. This screw caught his undershirt. The accident need not have happened if the company would only keep things to protect the workers from obvious dangers."

19.
Accident: Left arm crushed.
Name: I. M——.
Nationality: Polish.
Age: Sixteen.
Married or single: Single.

Establishment: Plant F.
Work: Laborer.
Date of accident: January 16, 1912.
Medical Attention: Dr. I. W——.

Statement of case: Was left an orphan with young sisters to care for, and went to work at Plant F. I. M—— had been working several months, when, in regular performance of his duties, an accident occurred which caused his left arm to be crushed. The physician sent him to the E—— Hospital where he remained nine weeks. His arm had to be amputated at the elbow. The boy, though small and undeveloped, is now in fairly good health. In September, 1912, he was awarded $2,000 on a suit against the company. He had sued for $30,000.

Statement of physician: ". . . I would not say that the company he worked for ought to give him any money for it."

Statement of boy: "I had to go to work to take care of my little sisters, and how was I to know how to protect myself from getting my arm hurt? Now it is gone and I can never work like a man could."

23.
Accident: Back and ribs broken; fatal.
Name: U. J——.
Nationality: Polish.
Age: Thirty-eight.
Married or single: Married. Three children.
Date of accident: July 16, 1912.
Establishment: Plant G.
Work: Laborer.
Date of Investigation: July 30, 1912.
Medical Attention: Dr. I. W——.

Statement of case: U. J—— had been in the United States only nine weeks when the accident occurred. He understood no English. He was help two other workmen to pile up bags of cement, and was injured by their falling on him and two others. His back and ribs were broken. He was taken to the E— Hospital.

Statement of physician: "U. J— has a chance to live but he will be partially paralyzed."

Note: U. J— died August 30, 1912.

QUESTIONS

1. Should the employers of these victims have borne any responsibility for these accidents? If so, in which instances?
2. What do these cases tell you about the state of medical care in the early 1910s? Do you think these workers got the best care possible at that time?
3. Should it be the responsibility of government to regulate workplaces to prevent accidents like these?

18

Machinist Orrin Cheney Testifies to Congress on the Taylor System of Shop Management, 1911

Frederick W. Taylor developed a system called scientific management around the turn of the twentieth century. By 1911, enough firms had mimicked his method of handling labor that it became widely known as "Taylorism" or the "Taylor System." The two outstanding traits of Taylorism were paying workers by output in order to get them to work harder and timing workers performing specific tasks so as to ensure that they did their jobs in the "one best way."

One of the first employers to use the Taylor System was the United States government arsenal in Watertown, Massachusetts. Efficiency experts versed in Taylor's ideas showed up one day and began timing the skilled machinists who made parts for the arsenal's guns. Here, machinist Orrin Cheney describes his first experience with this new production regime. This kind of resentment led to a strike at the arsenal in 1911, shortly after the experts arrived. Although the strike only lasted a week, it had a great impact on people's perception of scientific management.

The congressional hearings from which the testimony below is taken culminated in the passage of a law banning the Taylor System at federal employment sites. Nevertheless, many private employers, whose workers were not organized enough to resist, implemented Taylor's ideas at their workplaces during the 1910s and 1920s. Taylor's ideas are still very influential today.

Excerpt from "Taylorism and Other Systems of Shop Management," Hearings HS 62-B-1, U.S. House of Representatives, October 4, 1911, 22–25.

The CHAIRMAN [of the Congressional Committee]. Do you know something about the introduction of the Taylor or similar system of shop management at the arsenal?

Mr. CHENEY. I know something of it. I have worked under it.

The CHAIRMAN. Will you state, for the information of the committee, what information you have in connection with the introduction and operation of the Taylor system?

Mr. CHENEY. I was given a job, I started on it, and I got set up on the job and was working all right on it and this expert came down with his stop watch and said he wanted to take the time. I said I did not believe in [a] stop watch for me, and I did not propose to have it. He said I would have to have it, and so I let him do it. Well, he told me to put it up to another speed, a higher speed than I was running. I was running a pretty good speed, I thought, that would turn the work out and turn it out right.

The CHAIRMAN. That is he put the machine up at a higher speed?

Mr. CHENEY. He put the machine up at a higher speed. Well, I put it up at a higher speed and started. The work was a good deal rougher, but on this particular job it did not matter—the roughness—because it had to be finished in another machine. I had timed myself on this piece before he timed me. I knew just what I could turn out a piece in, at the speed I was running, to a second, taking in all the operation at once. He put the stopwatch on and gave me a time limit. It was $19^1/_2$ half minutes. I had turned the same piece out on the feed and speed I was running on in $19^1/_2$ minutes, and I was doing a better job. . . .

When he put it up at this other speed I had so much trouble with it that I had to work hard myself to hustle and keep in his limit, his premium limit. Then he went along and I got another job and I started. We had the machine speeded up to a very high speed and a lieutenant who was in charge of the shop came through the shop and just then my belt jumped off the pulley, and I told the lieutenant that I could not follow this man's instructions and do my work and do it properly. I told him that I never had a man tell me what speed and feed I should run my machine on. My work was always given to me. "Well," he said, "you have got one now." I said, "I see I have and I do not know how long I shall keep it." Well, I started working and in a few minutes the major came down and he started and said, "Cheney, I understand you refuse to carry out these instructions." I went to say something and he said. "Shut right up; you will carry out these instructions to a letter." . . . So I could not say any more, and I started in and tried to carry out the instructions, and the job was not passed by the inspector, and I had a card to fill out why it was not. I filled out the card and told him the reason why was because I did not have time to do it, and that was the last I heard of it. . . .

The CHAIRMAN. Will you tell the committee why it was that with the machine speeded up at greater speed, you were unable to get out the work any faster, and that when you did put it out that it did not pass inspection?

Mr. CHENEY. I had to water the tools more than what I did before, and I was doing it on a different speed. I was running a coarser speed in my way, then, I was on a faster speed, and there were little different things in the machine that I could overcome at a slower speed which I could not at a high speed. And the trouble I had with the belts—they would not stay on the machine—they kept jumping off. Then there was also the oiling up of the machine and different things.

The CHAIRMAN. Then before this timepiece was placed upon you, you had used your own judgement in relation to the speed?

Mr. CHENEY. I had used my own judgement.

The CHAIRMAN. When the timepiece was placed upon you, you had to use the judgement of the management as to the speed and feed?

Mr. CHENEY. I did. And the man who held the watch over me told me to put it up on a higher speed. He told me, he said, "I know nothing about this particular machine whatever."

QUESTIONS

1. Why did Cheney resent being timed? Was it just his difficulty with keeping up with the new limit or was there something more?
2. Why would management have been interested in raising the speed of the machines in the arsenal if higher speed meant that the workers produced parts that did not pass inspection?
3. Might Taylorism have been introduced into the Watertown Arsenal in a better way so that it might have been successful there?

The Union
Movement

*The Grand Demonstration of Workingmen
passing the reviewing stand at Union Square, New York, 1882.
No. WHi-10302, courtesy Wisconsin Historical Society.*

19

Initiation Ceremony of the Knights of Labor, ca. 1880

The Knights of Labor was the first national labor organization to embrace the principles of what is now known as "industrial unionism." Unlike the trade unions that preceded it, which organized workers on the basis of skill or "craft," the Knights of Labor organized all workers into one union, regardless of occupation.

Indeed, nearly all workers in any industry were eligible to join the Knights of Labor, even managers. This initiation ritual shows how the Knights of Labor represented a middle ground between fraternal organization and labor union. It also demonstrates the importance of a cultural framework for keeping the union together.

THE MASTER WORKMAN* will direct the Unknown Knight to go to the Vestibule and obtain the names and occupations of the candidates in waiting, return to the Assembly, and report to the M. W. If the candidates reported are indorsed by the Recording Secretary as having been duly proposed, balloted for and elected, he (*or she*) will return to the vestibule and make the prescribed examination. If the examination is satisfactory, he (*or she*) will announce to the Inside Esquire, who will announce them to the M. W., who will direct them to be admitted. The U. K. will proceed to the opening in the circle, and introduce them to the M. W., who will order the candidates to be placed at the centre and the pledge administered and the Initiation proceeded with as per usage.

Excerpt from [Terence Powderly], *Adelphon Kruptos.* (ca. 1880), 11–24.
*In the original text, all officers in the union are referred to only by initials. To clarify the document while remaining true to the original, the officer names will be spelled out in the first reference only.

M. W. Does any one know cause why the candidate (or candidates) should not be covered with our shield and admitted into our Order?

When any one may lawfully object by giving good reasons. The Assembly shall then consider the same, and a majority-vote shall decide. If no objections are made or sustained the M. W. shall proceed—

M. W. U. K., you will proceed to the vestibule and make the prescribed examination; if the candidates accept, deliver them at the centre for obligation.

The U. K. retires and propounds the following questions, to which the candidate (*or candidates*) must assent:—

U. K.: Do you believe in, and approve of, united effort for the betterment of mankind?

Candidate: I do.

U. K. Do you desire to engage in such an effort?

Candidate: I do.

U. K. Do you earn your bread by labor?

Candidate: I do.

U. K. Are you willing to bind yourself with a pledge of honor to SECRECY, OBEDIENCE AND MUTUAL ASSISTANCE?

Candidate: I am.

U. K. If you are admitted will you promptly attend to the little details necessary for the successful operation of the Assembly?

Candidate: I will.

U. K. Will you, if called to any position, perform the duties of that position faithfully?

Candidate: I will.

U. K. If appointed to a committee, will you, to the best of your ability, perform the task allotted to the committee?

Candidate: I will.

U. K. Will you retain your confidence in every officer and member until it is clearly proved that they are dishonest or unfit longer to remain in office?

Candidate: I will.

U. K. Will you step up to the desk of the Financial Secretary regularly every month and pay up your monthly dues, and if the interests of labor demand it, will you cheerfully pay any assessment levied on you?

Candidate: I will.

U. K. Will you keep the secrets of the organization and guard them as sacredly as you would your honor, bearing in mind that in betraying the secrets of an organization, you betray both your own and those of others; remembering that he (or she) who cannot keep his (or her) own secrets, is a fool, and he (or she) who betrays the secrets of others, is a traitor, and that of all mean creatures, nothing can be meaner than a treacherous fool?

Candidate. I will.

U. K. Will you form the resolution to stand by the organization through thick and thin; through good and ill report, and do your part toward pushing onward the wheel of Labor's emancipation—neither tiring nor faltering in your work? and will you, when no longer able to push the wheel, teach your children to take up the burden when you leave off, and struggle along in the path of human progress?

Candidate: I will.

U. K. You will then proceed with me to the centre, and assume the pledge of honor.

[The candidate takes the pledge of honor, and the Venerable Sage explains the Knights' secret handshakes and hand signals.]

U. K. Master Workman, our friend has (or friends have) been properly instructed in the workings of an Assembly, and by direction of the V. S., are now presented to you for final instruction.

M.W. "Labor is noble and holy." To defend it from degradation, to divest it of the evils to body, mind, and estate, which ignorance and greed have imposed; to rescue the toiler from the grasp of the selfish, is a work worthy of the noblest and best of our race. You have proved yourself willing to accept the responsibility, and to labor, with what ability you possess, for the triumph of these principles.

On behalf of the toiling millions of earth, I welcome you to this Order, pledged to the service of Humanity. Open and public associations having failed, after a struggle of centuries, to protect or advance the interest of labor, we have lawfully constituted this Assembly. Hid from public view, we are covered by a veil of secrecy, not to promote or shield wrong doing, but to shield ourselves and you from persecution and wrong by men in our own sphere and calling, as well as others out of it, when we endeavor to secure the just reward of our toil. In using the power of organized effort and co-operation, we but imitate the example of capital heretofore set in numberless instances. In all the multifarious branches of trade, capital has its combinations; and, whether intended or not, they crush the manly hopes of labor and trample poor humanity in the dust. We mean no conflict with legitimate enterprise, no antagonism to necessary capital; but, men, in their haste and greed, blinded by self-interests, overlook the interests of others, and sometimes violate the rights of those they deem helpless. We mean to uphold the dignity of labor, to affirm the dignity of all who earn their bread by the sweat of their brow. We mean to create a healthy public opinion on the subject of labor (the only creator of values), and the justice of its receiving a full, just share of the values or capital it has created. We shall, with all our strength, support laws made to harmonize the interest of labor and capital, for labor alone gives life and value to capital, and also those laws which tend to lighten the exhaustiveness of toil. We shall use every lawful and honorable means to procure and retain employ for one another, coupled with just and fair remuneration; and, should accident or misfortune befall any of our number, render such aid as lies within our power to give, without inquiring their country or creed; and without approving of general strikes among artisans, yet should it become justly necessary to enjoin an oppressor, we will protect and aid any of our members who thereby may suffer loss, and as opportunity offers, extend a helping hand to all branches of honorable toil.

QUESTIONS

1. To what extent does the ritual see labor as masculine? To what extent were the Knights gender-neutral?
2. Why do you think the Knights created such elaborate rituals?
3. Why do you think the Knights saw their philosophy as superior to ordinary trade unionism?

20

Anonymous, "Lines on the Homestead Riots: Wednesday, July 6th, 1892"

The Homestead Lockout of 1892 is important to American labor history for at least three reasons. First, it was instigated by a firm headed by Andrew Carnegie, one of the most successful businessmen in history, who just six years before had published words in praise of trade unions in a national magazine. Second, it greatly contributed to the collapse of trade unionism in the American iron and steel industry for approximately forty-five years. Third, it was one of the most violent incidents in American labor history. On July 6, 1892, seven workers and three Pinkerton guards died in a gunfight when the Pinkertons attempted to land along the Monongahela River outside Carnegie Steel's Homestead Works. They had been dispatched by management to protect replacements for the locked-out workers.

Here, an anonymous poet recalls the events of the gunfight. The poem does not match accounts and other evidence of the incident. Perhaps more important, it leaves out information such as the death of the Pinkertons and the beating the guards withstood at the hands of Homestead citizens after they surrendered to the force that met them at the banks. Nevertheless, one can learn much by examining how working people wanted their losses to be remembered by history.

Excerpt reproduced in David P. Demarest, Jr., ed., *"The River Ran Red": Homestead 1892* (Pittsburgh: University of Pittsburgh Press, 1992),103.

Night has cast its darkened mantle
    O'er the vale and mountain steep.
And the birds have ceased their warbling—
    In their nests they softly sleep.

By the moonbeam's glimmering radiance
    Forms are seen like phantoms bright,
Gliding to and fro with anxious
    Watchings through the lonesome night.

All along the river, sentinels
    Pace its banks with searching eye,
Ready to convey the signal,
    Should the foe be lurking nigh.

Whilst their vigilant task pursuing,
    Distant sounds break on the ear,
Wafted by the gentle breezes
    O'er the moonlit waters clear.

Look! it is the "Little Billy!"
    See the barges are in tow;
Sound the alarm, it is the enemy;
    Let the Homestead people know.

Quick along the wires flashing
    Speed the message of alarm:
"To arms! To arms! prepare to meet them;
    Make resistance—every man!"

Ready to obey their leaders
    Thousands rush with maddened haste,
'Till they reach the place of landing
    Where, in line, each man is placed.

Then speaks out a voice stentorian:
    "Men, remember, don't shoot first;
If 'Pinkerton' should force a landing,
    Bear the consequence they must."

The air is rent with cheers defiant
   As the barges heave in sight;
Every man is served for action,
   Should the foe persist to fight.

The barges reach the final landing
   Where the "warnings" are exchanged
By both leaders; each in turn
   The situation well explained.

Heedless of the doom awaiting,
   The leader gave his men command:
"Ready, march!" each man obeying,
   Made their first attempt to land.

Then a fierce and deadly conflict
   Throws a shadow o'er the scene:
Flash on flash, in quick secession,
   Mark the enemy's lines between.

The Pinkertons in scattered numbers,
   Are driven back in quick retreat;
Thrice they charge to gain the workshops
   Thrice they suffer sad defeat.

All day long the conflict rages;
   Night has brought its saddened tale;
In the morn lips red and rosy,
   Closed in death lies cold and pale.

Weeping mourners o'er their loved ones;
   Pitying eyes, tear—filled with grief;
Sympathizing hearts, with gracious
   Offerings seek to lend relief.

> Thus a day of strife has ended,
> Which in memory shall recall
> Scenes that ne'er can be forgotten
> Long as stands "Carnegie Hall."*

Questions

1. How do you know the author favored labor's position in the strike?
2. What was the author's purpose in writing the poem after the events of July 6, 1892?
3. Is the poem effective propaganda? Why or why not?

*Carnegie Hall is a concert hall in New York City constructed with money donated by Andrew Carnegie and named after him.

21

"Junius" Opposes American Imperialism, ca. 1898

Although a majority of Americans either favored annexing territories or were apathetic on the matter, a vocal minority opposed the creation of an American empire. Some anti-imperialists saw annexation of Hawaii and former Spanish colonies as a contradiction of the United States' historic role as the first colony to declare its independence from a ruling power, but most of them feared that inhabitants of the colonies would come to the United States, undermining the Anglo-Protestant character of the country.

Labor leaders were prominent in the movements to oppose imperialism and limit immigration to the United States. Mostly, union leaders feared competition from workers who did not come from countries with a tradition of union organization, and they believed that non-European people had unusual, in-born abilities to work long hours with little pay, food, or rest.

Dorman C. Eaton (1823–1899), an attorney and Republican reformer in New York City who wrote under the name Junius, brings these two strains together. Seeing Hawaiian annexation as a revival of slavery, Eaton fears its impact on American workers and farmers.

SLAVERY—CARRIED ON under the name of "contract" labor, . . . exists to-day in Hawaii. Under this system, sugar is made to compete with domestic sugar and in this way have the Hawaiian Islands been populated, by legislative appropriations. The natural conditions in the Sandwich Islands are against either white or common negro labor. It requires cold, hunger and ambition, or

Excerpt from Junius [Dorman B. Eaton], *Hawaiian Annexation and Our Labor Laws*, 3–4, 7, 9, 11.

9 6

the desire to excel, to induce work when they are not compelled to work by law, and these elements are missing in the labor system of Hawaii. Most of the English West India negroes won't work because they can live without work, a sweet potato and a banana making a full meal and clothing not necessary.

We do not quite see how New England Senators and Representatives, nor how any *Republican* in fact, can endorse this sort of slavery, even if it is called "contract" labor and is offered through "annexation." It certainly is quite as odious in *that* form as in any other.

It is a wonder that any Senator from Massachusetts—with her rememberance of Josiah Quincy, John Quincy Adams, Rufus Choate, Charles Sumner, Wendell Phillips, aye, and Daniel Webster, can favor annexing Hawaii with its "contract" labor.

[. . .]

What has become of their earlier professions concerning domestic slavery? Have the American people so soon forgotten the late war; have they counted its carnage and cost to free the black slaves! Is it consistent in the United States to so soon "annex" or take unto itself this Hawaiian system of semi-white slavery? Can the Republican party, with its professions in favor of well-paid and free labor, and with its past record on "contract" labor, *afford to carry the load* which this "annexation" scheme of a few foreign sugar planters is certain to put upon it! It would certainly raise an issue in this country of which the oppposition would not be slow to take advantage; a very dangerous issue, the settlement of which would either force the Hawaiian "Sugar Trust" to yield it or it would push the Republican party to the point of disruption! And all to aid a few foreign sugar planters who have already had of us $66,000,000 of sugar bounty!

In the Hawaiian Legislature of 1890 the second most important question forced to the front by the Hawaiian "Sugar Trust" in the Islands was that of "contract" or coolie labor. The sugar and rice planters had a pressing need for seven or eight thousand more laborers, and Japanese "contract" and Chinese coolie labor was regarded as the most available. The Legislature finally passed a law allowing the admission of more Chinese under a specific contract—amounting to little less than slavery, under bonds, etc., that they engage in nothing but sugar and rice planting!

[. . .]

Nature has provided that the principal or field labor in Hawaii cannot be done except by people suited to tropical climate—that is, not by whites. Government on a truly democratic basis is therefore out of the question. If the *outward form* of a "republic" be preserved, it can be only an oligarchy far more pronounced and exclusive than any in our Southern States was, becuase the proportion of white people is smaller.

The oligarchy well knows that *white* labor cannot stand work in any country where the sugar-cane will grow. From Port-au-Prince to Penang the cane-fields have always been fatal to whites. Since the sugar supply came from Barbary until now, only natives of the tropics or a high mixture of native blood with the Latin races, or Asiatics have been able to stand the humid heat in which sugar is developed in the cane.

The Scotch-Darien Company found this out to its sorrow a century and a half ago, and it is as well settled from the Teche sugaries of Louisiana to the malaria-smitten mills of Manilla as any physical fact developed by human experience. Hawaiian cane plantations, now infested by Chinese and Japanese coolies to the number of about 40,000, re-enforced by innumerable half and quarter castes from the islands of the sea, cannot be worked successfully by white labor from California.

[. . .]

This Hawaiian "annexation" scheme overturns the very pedestal upon which rests a vital principle of the Republican party and of all our labor organizations! Mr. Geo. W. Merrill, of California, who was our Minister to the Hawaiian Islands only a few years ago, frankly says—

"The Eastern people, who desire the annexation of Hawaii, have little idea *what such a step means for this nation.* It is the height of folly for Congress to consider laws to check undesirable immigration from Europe and to close the Pacific coast to Chinese and then *at one fell swoop* admit some 77,000 Hawaiians, Chinese, and Japanese to the benefits of this matchless Republic. That clause in the proposed treaty about debarring Chinese residents of Hawaii from coming to this country *is a blind.* How can any law be constitutional that bars residents of one Territory or State from entering another? We shall simply give citizenship to more Chinese than there are now in San Francisco, besides thousands of vile offscourings of a half dozen other nations. If I were the owner of sugar plantations on the Hawaiian Islands, or a San Francisco merchant and shipper dealing with Hawaii, I would rejoice at the proposed annexation. In fact *they are all at the bottom of this annexation "scheme,"* but how *other* people can wish it is beyond my comprehension."

Here we have the whole matter in a nutshell, and strange as it may seem, the American people have not come to see it!

QUESTIONS

1. To what extent did labor leaders take the same view of immigration as Eaton does? How were workers' concerns different?
2. Eaton clearly loathed the idea of returning to a slavery economy. However, to what extent does his rejection of slavery add up to racial tolerance?
3. What do you think Hawaiian sugar-plantation workers' views of annexation were? Why do you think so?

22

Pearl Jolly Recalls the Ludlow Massacre, 1916

The Colorado mining industry gave rise to some of the most violent incidents in American labor history around the turn of the twentieth century. A series of strikes at that time culminated in the infamous Ludlow Massacre of 1914. Colorado State Militiamen turned machine guns on and torched a tent colony of women and children of workers striking to get the Colorado Fuel and Iron Company (CF&I), the largest mining firm in the state, to recognize their union, the United Mine Workers of America (UMW).

Here, Mrs. Pearl Jolly, a survivor of the Massacre, describes the massacre to the federal Commission on Industrial Relations, which chose to investigate the incident as part of its charge to examine ways to improve relations between labor and capital. Her extremely one-sided account helped put pressure on CF&I and its chief stockholder, John D. Rockefeller, Jr., to improve labor relations in the industry so as to prevent further violence. In response to the massacre, Rockefeller instigated the implementation of what came to be known as the Rockefeller Plan, the first important company-dominated union designed to give workers a voice in the workplace and eliminate the need for independent representation. Because of the plan, it took until 1933 for the UMW to win a contract at CF&I.

THEY PUT GUARDS in our camps Sunday night to take care of the camp, but nothing happened. On the following Monday morning, about 9 o'clock, [five militiamen] came to the Ludlow grounds.

Excerpt from United States Commission on Industrial Relations, *Final Report and Testimony,* Volume 7, 64th Congress, 1st Session, Document No. 415, 1916, 6347–54.

They had a paper and they sent in for Louis Tikas, a Greek and the leader; they handed him this slip of paper, and it had some foreign name on it of some man that was not in the tent colony; they asked him if they had a warrant or had been sent there by the civil authorities. They said no, they had been sent there by the military authorities. . . . When they met Louis Tikas they went and called up Manager Hemrock and and asked him if he would see him and talk to him. He said he would. They met at the C.&S. depot. I don't know what the conversation was at the depot, but I know when Louis [T]ikas came back he told us the machine guns and everything were set ready to wipe the tent colony. The next thing we observed was Louis Tikas coming from the depot waiving a white handkerchief. There were about 200 tents in the tent colony in front in large groups. He was waiving the white handkerchief, I suppose, for us to get back. While he was running toward us and waiving the white handkerchief they fired two bombs. Following that they turned the machine gun into the tent colony and started to firing with rifles. Our men decided if they would take the hills, take their rifles and go into the hills and thus protect the women and children in the tent colony. There was just 40 rifles in the Ludlow camp. They will tell you there was 500 or so. There was 40 in there, and I would swear that before any jury in the United States. The men who had rifles went into the hills, and the others, too, so that there would not be any men in the camp, thinking in that way they would attract the fire away from the women and children. Then if no men were there they would not fire. They did not follow the men into the hills; they were too cowardly; they wanted to fight with the women. They kept the machine guns turned on the camp all day, more or less. The women and children, too, could run out of the camp, but there were so many women there expecting to become mothers, and also many that had such a large family of small children that they could not possibly get out. . . .

[I]t was terrible the way those bullets came in there; it does not seem possible to tell how they were coming in. They would say if the bullets were coming in like that, why were there not more shot? Simply because the caves were there and the dogs and chickens and everything else that moved were shot. Between 5 and 6 o'clock they set fire to our tents. When they set fire to our tents we decided that we would go from cave to cave as fast as we could. They could see us going through, and we had to dodge their bullets. . . . The screams of the women and children—they were simply awful. When [Louis Tikas] was on his way to the cave they captured him and took him prisoner. After they took him prisoner, they couldn't decide for a little while how they wanted to kill him. Some contended to shoot him; some contended that he should be hanged. Finally, Lieut. Linderfeldt went up and hit him over the head with a rifle, broke the butt of the gun over his head, and then made the remark he spoiled a good gun on him.

They stepped on his face. We have a photograph. I don't believe we have it here, but it shows plain the prints of the heel in his face. After he fell, he was shot four times in the back. . . .

On Wednesday they told me that they found 700 guns—and it is just such outraqgeous stories as that they tell on the miners in this case, and you have simply got to judge them yourselves. They told me they had 700 guns and 10,000 rounds of ammunition in [union leader] John R. Lawson's tent. And one of the first tents to burn down on Monday was the Lawson[s'] Now, that is the story told. Now, if there had been 700 guns in that tent, gentlemen, I tell you here, there would not have been quite so many have come through that day—that is, the militia. If our men had had 100 guns they could have protected us and there would not have been so many women and children slaughtered. But they did not have nothing, and they couldn't get anything. The militia had taken up all our guns and given them to the mine guards. They had, every one of their men—we speak of the guards as scabs—with their guns and revolvers two weeks before, and had them at the mines there. And this corporation there, they were taking these men out, these strike breakers, and taking them to Trinidad [Colorado, near Ludlow] and giving commissions allowing them to carry a revolver; and at the time of this battle these men all had commissions and were armed, and our men didn't have anything and couldn't get anything. I think that is about all my experience.

QUESTIONS

1. Do you believe Mrs. Jolly's story? Why or why not?
2. Can shooting at a tent colony of women and children ever be justified, even if the first shot did come from there?
3. Should the management of the Colorado Fuel and Iron company, in particular John D. Rockefeller, Jr., have been held responsible for the actions of the Colorado National Guard?

Working-Class Culture

Workers in front of a new I.W.W. Hall
which replaced one burned by vigilantes.
No. WHi-10301, courtesy Wisconsin Historical Society.

An Agent for the United States Immigration Commission Describes the Working Life of Prostitutes, ca. 1909

For women around the world who sought a new life in America, the journey to the United States was filled with dangers. Along with the crowded conditions that all immigrants faced on ocean-going ships, young women faced the additional danger of being forced into prostitution, generally because of false promises of marriage from American men. With no marketable skills, it was also easier for young women to be exploited by "employers" who treated them like slaves.

These four women's stories show how experiences of Japanese, Jewish, and French women involved similar patterns of promise, deception, and degradation. As sympathetic to immigrants as these accounts look today, the commission organized to take these testimonies had the goal of restricting immigration altogether. The immigration restriction movement claimed ultimate success in 1924.

AFFIDAVIT OF AGENT OF [THE UNITED STATES] IMMIGRATION COMMISSION

A JAPANESE GIRL, aged 16, was brought into the United States via Canada, through Victoria, and taken to Bellingham, Wash., in the spring of 1908. She was sent from Japan as a proxy wife to meet her husband, who was a Japanese laborer in America. The husband was represented at the immigration station by a Japanese interpreter who is known to be a Japanese procurer. At the im-

Excerpt from United States Immigration Commission, *Report on Harboring Women for Immoral Purposes* (Washington, DC, Government Printing Office, 1910), 52–54.

migration station the Japanese whose wife she was said to be met her and the couple were married in the presence of the immigration authorities, —— [name stricken from affadavit] vouching for the husband's standing and character. The husband took the wife to Bellingham, Wash., and lived with her for several days in a rooming house which was occupied principally by prostitutes; the husband then left the woman and she was immediately taken charge of by a Japanese woman who managed a house of prostitution near by. At the end of two weeks' time the woman who ran the house of prostitution took the young wife to Seattle and sold her to a proprietor of a disorderly house named ——. The woman in Bellingham attempted to break the girl into the life of a prostitute; the girl refused to enter the life, and the woman beat her and starved her, which treatment continued during the entire time of two weeks. At the end of the two weeks the woman, realizing that she could not manage the girl, took her to Seattle and sold her, as above stated, for $1,600. ——, who bought the girl, made the purchase with the intention of sending the girl to Alaska, and the woman from Bellingham was to deliver the girl on the boat about to leave for Alaska. The $1,600 was to cover all expenses of importing the girl from Japan, the expense of the proxy marriage, including the price paid the Japanese who acted as husband, and all expenses of the delivery of the girl on board the boat for Alaska. The girl was taken to Alaska and placed in a house of prostitution. She rebelled up to the time the boat started and wept and fell upon her knees on the dock, begging not to be sent. The woman from Bellingham, who spoke English, forced the girl onto the boat and then explained to the officers of the boat that the girl was her daughter and did not wish to leave because she had a lover in Bellingham.

The truth concerning the entire case was not discovered until after the girl had sailed for Alaska.

Another girl, Polish Jew, aged 17, entered the United States through the Ellis Island port, booked for Montana. The procurer in this case was a Jew, and got this girl near the border of Russia by promises of marriage after they reached the United States. At the immigration station he gave their names as man and wife. He took the girl directly from New York to Montana, and broke her into the life there. He put her in a crib, and forced her to lead the life of a prostitute. They stayed in —— about six weeks, and then he took her to Seattle, Wash., and put her in the crib house of which ——, a Japanese, is the proprietor, and in which there are Japanese, Jewish, and French women as inmates. He kept her there about a month, and then moved her to the —— House, a house of prostitution of French and Jewish inmates. At the time he placed her in the —— House the girl was about two and a half months pregnant. Up to this time she had hoped that the man would marry her. When he found out that she was pregnant he refused to marry her, but made her work as an inmate in the house of prostitution daily, and collected all her money; he refused to give her any street clothes, and made her continue to work during her pregnancy and up to the time she went to the hospital. She did not go to the hospital until the day before her child was born. She was forced to continue her work when she was too ill to walk, and suffered terrible pain. The man refused to give her any money, and she went to a charitable hospital. While she was in the hospital, the man took another prostitute and left Washington for Butte, Mont. . . .

Another girl, French, aged 15, was working in Paris in a factory. On her way home, one evening, she met with a man and woman who spoke to her and asked her into a drinking place to have something warm. She went, and they told her she was unusually pretty and that they had a young man friend whom they would like to have her meet. The next night they met her again and had with them the young man. The young man made love to her and accomplished her ruin—after which she left her parents and never returned to them. The man put her on the streets of Paris. She became pregnant and continued to work as a prostitute until the end of six months' pregnancy. The man took care of her and after her child was born persuaded her to leave Paris and come to America with some friends of his who were in Paris. She did not want to leave her child, but did so and came to America with these friends. They took her to Chicago and she was there turned over by the —— to a man who took her to Butte, Mont. She lived with this man in Butte, Mont., for about a year, turning over all of her earnings to him; then she discovered that while she was giving him all her money from her earnings in a crib he was treating parlor-house girls to wine. Violent disagreements then arose between them and she was finally placed in jail for stabbing him. After her time was served she left Butte and went to Seattle, where she has since practiced prostitution, but has at no time given any of her earnings to a man. From her earnings she has been sending money to Paris to care for and educate her child. At the present time she is in ——, ——, where she has two houses of prostitution, one with four inmates and the other with three inmates. She does not practice prostitution herself at the present time.

QUESTIONS

1. Why did the women in these accounts stick with the men who forced them into becoming prostitutes?
2. How are the three women's experiences similar and different from each other?
3. In what ways do the experiences of these women resemble or differ from those of other workers?

24

Margaret Byington Studies the Diet of Steelworkers and Their Families, 1910

Most working men had women at home who helped make life bearable. The home, unlike the workplace, was a place where male workers could exercise some control over their lives. However, that control was far from complete. Wives had substantial influence in the way family life operated, particularly at mealtime. And, even then, the influence of employers could still be felt (by them determining the husband's hours of employment, for example).

Margaret Byington was one of a team of sociologists who examined many aspects of workplace life in a series of studies known as the Pittsburgh Survey. Her subject was the home lives of working-class steelworkers in Homestead, a suburb of Pittsburgh dominated by the United States Steel Corporation's Homestead steel mill. Here, Byington discusses how the wives of steelworkers planned and executed meals in Homestead, including some of the constraints with which they had to reckon.

DURING MY SOJOURNINGS in Homestead, I found it of little avail to stand knocking at front doors. It was wise to go straight to the back door, which opened into the warm and cheerful kitchen. Here I was sure to find the housekeeper busy preparing for the ever recurring meal, economically her most important task. Not only is food the largest item in the family account, but it is also one which, by thrift and ability, housewives can reduce without lessening the comfort of the family. The "cost of living" is a prob-

Excerpt from Margaret Byington, *Homestead: The Households of a Mill Town* (New York: Charities Publication Committee, 1910), 63–65.

lem they themselves are studying practically, and many of them took a lively interest in the results of the budget investigation.

In general, the account books revealed a fairly intelligent choice of foods, including a large amount of fruit and green vegetables, chosen apparently to meet the need of men who do very hot work. The following bill of fare for four days is fairly typical of the English-speaking households. The head of the family in this instance earned about $3.00 a day.

MONDAY

Breakfast: Oat-meal and milk, eggs and bacon, bread, butter, jelly, coffee.

Dinner: Soup, bread, fruit.

Supper: Meat, beans, potatoes, fruit, red beets, pickles.

TUESDAY

Breakfast: Chocolate, eggs, bread, butter, and jelly.

Dinner: Spinach, potatoes, pickles, warmed over meat, fruit, bread, butter.

Supper: Meat, sweet potatoes, carrots, beans, tomatoes, tea, bread, butter and fruit.

WEDNESDAY

Breakfast: Eggs, corncakes, potatoes, coffee, rhubarb, bread, butter.

Dinner: Soup, bread, butter.

Supper: Lamb stew with dumplings, cucumber, eggplant, beans, corn, coffee, bread and butter, fruit.

THURSDAY

Breakfast: Eggs, fruit, eggplant, coffee, cakes.

Dinner: Soup, bread and butter, cakes, fruit.

Supper: Fish, potatoes, tomatoes, cucumbers, pie, tea.

When the man does not come home for the noon meal, as in this instance, it is usually a light one for the rest of the household. In another family where they had eggs for breakfast and meat for supper, the children were fed at mid-day on mush and milk with bread and molasses.

In mill-town economics, the dinner pail must be reckoned with as part of the table, and a bill of fare must be read with that in mind. I was struck with the pains often taken with the "mister's" bucket. The women used to carry hot lunches to the mill, but they are not now allowed inside without a pass. Most of the men, as they are not given regular time for eating, snatch a bite between tasks, though some, whose work permits, stop for a leisurely meal. I even heard of men who took steaks to cook on the hot plates about the machines. But they usually rely on a cold meal, and the women take great pains to make it appetizing, especially by adding preserves in a little cup in a corner of the bucket. They try to give the man what he likes the most apparently half from pity at the cold food and hard work that fall to his lot.

On the other hand, the women do not seem to realize that special care is needed in feeding the children, and generally give them much the same that their elders have. The mothers rarely attempt to check the natural tendency of childhood to be always running in for a bite between meals. The children suffer, too, from the fact that the time for meals is irregular because of the weekly change in the man's hours. One woman told me that the men get a bad habit of eating at odd times in the mill, and with this and meal hours changing every week, expect to eat whenever they feel like it. The household naturally picks up the habit with disastrous results both to digestion and housekeeping.

Sunday dinner is the one meal that serves as a time of festivity. Almost every account showed that on Saturday an extra piece of meat, usually a roast, was bought. The men have some leisure on Sunday and sit down with pleasure to a more elaborate dinner. Sometimes the married sons and daughters come home for that meal, and altogether it plays a part in the week's pleasure. Unfortunately, however, as the men usually work either Saturday night or Sunday night, they rarely have the whole Sunday to themselves, with that sense of freedom and let-up which means so much at the end of the week.

Occasionally, especially on holidays, there are family reunions. On Thanksgiving, when the mills run as usual, few preparations are made for the harried dinner. Christmas, however, is a great day in Homestead. Twice a year, on that day and on July

Fourth, the great mill stops. Everybody who can goes home, some to families in Homestead, others to neighboring towns, and there are Christmas trees in many homes. Some of the women who kept budget accounts took care to explain that their unusual expenses in December, both for food and extras, were for Christmas festivities.

Formal guests are infrequent. Where the housewife is also cook, there are difficulties in the way of hospitality, which are accentuated by the irregular meals and the hours of work. People who live simply and eat informally rarely utilize the meal time for guests as do more conventional households. But though rarely a time of festivity, the meal time is always present in the housewife's mind. When asked for an account of what they spent on food the women usually responded cheerfully, "We spend all we can get." They realized, nevertheless, that economies are possible and necessary if bills are to be met on pay day. For in spite of the reputed high wages among steel workers, the problem Homestead housewives face in trying to provide food and a good home on a man's earnings is no easy one.

QUESTIONS

1. Did the people of Homestead eat well compared to working-class people today? How are you defining the term *well?* Would using a different definition change your answer?
2. How did the conditions of work the father faced affect the eating habits of the family?
3. Is power over food purchase and preparation a sign of women's influence or their constraint?

25

Werner Sombart Analyzes "The Democratic Style of Public Life in America," 1906

As discussed in the introduction to this part, Americans in the late nineteenth and early twentieth centuries frequently debated what could be done to promote labor stability in changing economic times. While some answered the labor question with incremental reforms, others argued that the labor question had already been answered.

Pioneering German sociologist Werner Sombart (1863–1941), in his most famous work, offered a common answer to the labor question. In his Why is there no Socialism in the United States? *Sombart answers his question by examining organizational structure and compensation patterns in American factories, American workers' propensity for starting their own businesses and thus moving out of the strict definition of* worker, *and, as below, how Americans behaved in public.*

IT IS NOT ONLY in his position vis-à-vis the material world (that is, in his material standard of living) that the American worker is so much more favored than his European counterpart. In his relations to people and to social institutions, and in his position in and to society—in short, in what I call his social position—the American is also better-off than he would be in the contrasting European situation. For him 'Liberty' and 'Equality' (not only in the formal political sense but also in the economic and social sense) are not empty ideas and vague dreams, as they are for the

English translation copyright © 1976 by Patricia M. Hocking and C. T. Husbands. Excerpt from Werner Sombart, *Why is there no Socialism in the United States?* (Armonk, NY: M. E. Sharpe, 1976), pp. 109–110. Reprinted with permission.

European working class; for the most part they are realities. The American's better social position is largely the result of his political position and his economic situation—of a radical-democratic system of government and a comfortable standard of living. Both these are to be found within a colonizing population with no history, which basically consisted, and still does consist, wholly of immigrants; a population in which there are no feudal institutions, except in some Southern slave states.

Unfortunately, it is not possible to determine the nature of this social position of the worker as exactly was the case with his political and economic situation, either with the help of sections of the law or of numbers. Demonstration has to rest partly on intuitions, it has to be satisfied with the assessment of symptoms, and it should not underestimate details; yet it will still remain incomplete overall. The general impression must then replace what exact proof cannot demonstrate.

Anyone who has ever observed, even only fleetingly, male and female American workers as they carry on their life outside the factory or the workshop, has noticed on first sight that they are a different breed of people from German workers. We saw earlier how smartly and frequently elegantly clothed the workers are, especially the female ones, as they go on their way to work. On the street they are like members of the middle class and they act as working gentlemen and working ladies. In the external appearance of the American worker there is not the stigma of being in the class apart that almost all European workers have about them. In his appearance, in his demeanor, and in the manner of his conversation, the American worker also contrasts strongly with the European one. He carries his head high, walks with a lissom stride, and is as open and cheerful in his expression as any member of the middle class. There is nothing oppressed or submissive about him. He mixes with everyone—in reality and not only in theory—as an equal. The trade-union leader taking part in a ceremonial banquet moves with the same self-assurance on the dance floor as would any aristocrat in Germany. However, he also wears a finely fitting dress suit, patent-leather boots and elegant clothes of the latest fashion, and so, even in his appearance, nobody can distinguish him from the President of the Republic.

The bowing and scraping before the 'upper classes', which produces such an unpleasant impression in Europe, is completely unknown. It does not occur to a waiter, or to a street-car conductor, or to a policeman, to behave differently when he is confronted by an ordinary worker than he would if he had the Governor of Pennsylvania in front of him. That produces a spirit of self-respect, both in the person who behaves in this way, and in the one to whom the behaviour is directed if he belongs to the poorer population.

The whole of public life has a more democratic style. The worker is not being reminded at every turn that he belongs to a 'lower' class. Indicative of this is the one class of carriage on all railways (which just lately is beginning to be done away with because of the advent of Pullman cars).

Snobbery about personal status is also less common in the United States than in Germany in particular. It is not what one is and still less what one's parents were that decide one's prestige, but what one accomplishes, and for that reason the very word 'work' in its abstract form is made into an honorary title. Thus, even the worker is treated respectfully, although—or rather because—he is only a worker. It is therefore natural that he feels differently from his counterpart in a country where a person only begins to be considered a person when he is, if not a baron, then a reserve officer, a doctor, or a person on probation for a profession.

Because of the democratic system of government, universal education, and the higher standard of living of the worker, there is genuinely a lesser social distance between the individual strata of the population, and—due to the effect of the customs and perceptions described—this distance becomes even smaller in the consciousness of the various classes than it really is.

QUESTIONS

1. Would Sombart's observations hold true today?
2. Sombart is mainly talking about white, male workers in this passage. How would his ideas apply to African Americans? To women workers? To people recently arrived in the United States from Europe and Asia?
3. In addition to Sombart's ideas in this excerpt, why do you think there was no socialism in the United States?

26

Joe Hill, "The Preacher and the Slave," 1911

Joe Hill was a Swedish immigrant who wrote song lyrics for the Industrial Workers of the World (IWW). Formed in 1905, the "Wobblies" were undoubtedly the most radical trade union in the history of the United States. Unlike mainstream labor organizations, the IWW was committed to destroying the capitalist system.

These lyrics were often parodies of popular songs of the time. They were passed on from worker to worker, sometimes embellished and changed along the way. Although he was known only for his lyrics during his lifetime, when Utah authorities executed Hill for murder in 1915 he became a labor legend.

"The Preacher and the Slave" pokes fun at religious figures who tried to prevent workers from fighting for better pay. Many versions exist. This one comes from an IWW songbook that the United States government used as an exhibit to convict IWW leaders of treason during World War I. The "starvation army" in line 9 is a reference to the Salvation Army, a religious charity whose workers still ring bells outside stores every Christmastime.

([SUNG TO THE] TUNE [OF]: "SWEET BYE AND BYE")

Long-haired preachers come out every night,
Try to tell you what's wrong and what's right;
But when asked how 'bout something to eat
They will answer with voices so sweet:

Excerpt from "I.W.W. Songs to Fan the Flames of Discontent," University of Arizona Special Collections AZ 114 box 1, folder 1A, exhibit 27, http://digital.library.arizona.edu/bisbee/docs/027.php#PREACH.

CHORUS
You will eat, bye and bye,
In that glorious land above the sky;
Work and pray live on hay,
You'll get pie in the sky when you die.

And the starvation army they play,
And they sing and they clap and they pray.
Till they get all your coin on the drum,
Then they'll tell you when you're on the bum:

Holy Rollers and jumpers come out,
And they holler, they jump and they shout.
"Give your money to Jesus," they say,
"He will cure all diseases today."

If you fight hard for children and wife—
Try to get something good in this life—
You're a sinner and bad man, they tell,
When you die you will sure go to hell.

Workingmen of all countries, unite,
Side by side we for freedom will fight:
When the world and its wealth we have gained
To the grafters we'll sing this refrain:

LAST CHORUS
You will eat, bye and bye,
When you've learned how to cook and to fry
Chop some wood, 'twill do you good,
And you'll eat in the sweet bye and bye.

QUESTIONS

1. Is this song anti-religion? Why or why not?
2. Does religion help or hurt workers involved in a class struggle?
3. Why would workers sing this song? How would doing so help IWW members or workers in general?

27

Francis H. McClean Reports on the Amusements of the Bowery, 1899

The historian Lawrence Levine has written memorably about the division between "highbrow" and "lowbrow" culture that first surfaced in the United States during the late nineteenth century. Shakespeare, for example, once had a multiclass audience across the United States. By this time, however, the working-class audience had developed other theatrical interests. While Broadway remained the home of traditional theater, the center of working-class and ethnic theater became the Bowery, a raucous neighborhood near New York's Lower East Side immigrant district. The Bowery was the birthplace of vaudeville, which had an immeasurable impact on the evolution of modern mass culture.

In 1899, Francis H. McClean reported on Bowery theater for the University Settlement Society of New York. Settlement societies like this one McClean worked for organized houses in working-class neighborhoods in an attempt to improve the lives of the urban poor. Part of the mission of the settlement houses was to enlighten the poor by teaching them upper-class manners and exposing them to highbrow culture. As far as McLean was concerned, Bowery theaters were the competition. Thanks to reformers like him, Bowery amusements were driven out of the neighborhood in the years immediately preceding World War I.

THE BOWERY MARKS the western boundary of the great Hebrew section and the eastern boundary of the land of the Italians. But in

Excerpt from Francis H. McLean, "Bowery Amusements," *Year Book of the University Settlement Society of New York, 1899* (New York: The Winthrop Press, 1899), 14–19.

itself it is quite distinct in character from either. This is because it is the street of amusement for all of the lower East Side, and for that reason has a general air of rough cosmopolitanism about it. It numbers among its habitues the great lodging-house population, estimated to be about 40,000, composed of the waifs and strays of all nations; a population which, though constantly shifting and changing, remains an ever-present force, especially in times of political need. Many of these homeless men are earning honest livelihoods by hard labor—others are simply tramps living by their wits. They are all men whom life's vicissitudes have coarsened. Add to these the unending stream of the curious minded out for a good time; soldiers and sailors, boys showing the town to their guests, occasional slum parties, and other flotsam and jetsam of that sort. And, again, add to these Irish, German, and Hebrew contingents—and you can picture the conglomeration of men to whom the Bowery is the Mecca for pleasure. The word "men" is used advisedly, for, so far as amusements are concerned, the Bowery is a man's street. There is, however, one exception to that statement. The Hebrew theaters are essentially family resorts. But outside of these, comparatively few respectable women are found in the places of amusement. Nor are there really many of the other sort, the demimonde, except in the music halls and along the street itself. It is chiefly the single man with money whom the Bowery amusement places endeavor to attract. . . .

Apart from the Hebrew resorts, which are to be discussed separately, we find there are two theaters to be considered. Up to the present year there were three, but since then one of them has been given over to the Hebrews. Cheap variety is now about the only staple of the American Bowery theater. Time was, and not so very far back, when the spectacular melodrama, lurid, coarse grained, and silly at times, but always essentially sound in its ethical teachings, was popular. But it appears to have had its day. Now it is the "smart" thing which goes. There is not much to be said in favor of the cheap variety show, either on the Bowery or elsewhere in the city. It is all of the same cheap and sometimes nasty character. The wit is of a dull and sodden sort, and when it treads on forbidden ground it is brutishly vile in innuendo. There is a healthy mixture of acrobats, gymnasts, jugglers, etc., which give tone to an otherwise stupid and often vulgar performance. Of course, it must be understood that there is no lack of passably nice looking girls, of bright-colored garments, of pretty dances, of good stage effects, and so on. But the one great danger in this sort of performance is that it does not lift the audiences a whit above the thoughts and feelings of their daily monotonous lives—except at rare intervals—on the contrary, many of them have a distinct tendency to pull the auditors still further down into the mire. It is realism in art, with the idealistic element entirely expelled, and in its place an exaggeration of the bad, and the flippant, and the silly. Take for instance the comic sketches which have a little plot running through them. The manners and tempers of the characters in the play are of the sort which throw to the winds all thoughts of gentle or truly manly or womanly feeling. Coarseness and vulgarity are added to the horse play, which might be amusing in itself if not so complicated. . . . To anyone who may have had his sensibilities shocked by what has preceded, they may appear to be mere claptrap, and the applause which they receive simply trumpety enthusiasm. But, really, they show soundness of heart—which is encouraging. Of course, the drift toward the variety show in the Bowery theaters is but indicative of a drift which is evident throughout the dramatic field in New York. The tendency is everywhere toward the light, the very light. What that tendency means, what it will lead to, and exactly in what form the reaction will come, are questions far beyond the scope of this paper. Before closing it should be noted that the prices in the theaters range from ten to fifty cents. Beer is sold, but most of the drinking is done at the bars. Very few women, even of the demimonde, go to them. . . .

To pass to the Hebrew theaters is to pass into the clean atmosphere of a family resort. Whole families go to these places, the younger children often being seated two or three in one chair. Light edibles are brought and eaten between the acts, for the plays are generally very long. To glance over the audiences at these theaters, especially of the "sweller" one of the three, makes you appreciate the coming influence which the descendants of the immigrant Jew are going to have on many affairs. The younger generations have the same fire and vigor of their race stamped in their faces as of yore, but, added to it, an indefinable expression which indicates that the free play of American institutions has already had an effect. As to the plays, they are given in the Yiddish dialect—the Hebrew dialect of the East Side—which is a mixture of German and Hebrew. The same restless tendency which has affected the American theater in general is beginning to show itself in these race theaters. A few years back plays founded upon biblical subjects, or upon some incidents connected with the history of the race during the middle ages, were popular. Now comedy is in demand, and besides modern plays . . . are being translated into Yiddish for immediate use. It has been prophesied that eventually the variety show would even invade these sacred precincts.

QUESTIONS

1. What does McClean's attitude toward Bowery Theater suggest about class divisions between settlement-house workers and New York's immigrant population?
2. Would theatergoers in the Bowery agree with McLean's assessment of their variety shows? Do you think they wanted their entertainment "vulgar" and "light," or might they have a different view of the performances?
3. Why would Jewish immigrant members of the working class need theaters of their own?

Part III: 1914–1945

THE PERIODS OF AND THAT BETWEEN the two World Wars were marked by both suffering and opportunity for American labor. The lives of most white-collar workers, those who worked as managers or in offices, improved dramatically during this era. This was particularly true during the 1920s, when a booming stock market and the increased availability of high-cost consumer goods like cars and refrigerators changed many people's lives for the better. However, blue-collar workers—those who worked for wages in jobs that required physical strength or mechanical skill—did not fare so well. Mobilization for both world wars created blue-collar jobs, but the union-busting 1920s and the depression decade of the 1930s saw high levels of blue-collar unemployment.

When World War I began in 1914, the United States was not involved. Nevertheless, American workers benefited by getting high-paying jobs in industries that supplied war goods to the belligerent European nations. When the United States entered the war in 1917, that prosperity accelerated. With immigration from Europe shut off by the conflict, rural whites and African Americans began to move to cities in large numbers to take these war jobs. Government pressure to keep producing contributed to large gains in unionization and improvements in working conditions for industries mobilized for war. When the war ended, however, employers provoked a strike wave that rolled back gains in many industries, especially coal mining and steelmaking.

Skilled workers saw their income and their buying-power rise during the 1920s. However, their circumstances did not improve nearly as much as those of wealthy Americans. Less-skilled workers suffered from an excess of labor caused by mechanization and continued migration to the cities where most factories were located. Under these circumstances, the conditions that industrial workers faced grew increasingly difficult, especially for those in nonunion industries (see number 29, Williams). Many workers came to resent the role that government forces, both laws and law enforcement, played in keeping them from changing these conditions (see number 35, Muste).

For some segments of the labor force, depression started early. Agricultural wage workers, mostly members of minority groups, had no good times during this period unless they left the farm. Those who stayed faced the same kinds of dire conditions that had existed since the end of the Civil War (see number 30, Taylor).

The economic expansion associated with World War I and World War II benefited skilled industrial workers the most. But for many, these gains were only temporary. Union miners and machinists often lost their contracts in the 1920s. Although "Rosie the Riveter" was a symbol of women workers' strength during World War II, male workers often objected to working alongside women (see number 31, Gotzion). Furthermore, employers frequently fired women after the war ended when male workers returned from overseas. Government disapproval of strikes during wartime contributed to great gains in the number of workers represented by unions during both these conflicts. However, the National Labor Relations Act, one of a series of laws enacted as part of President Franklin Roosevelt's New Deal, did the most to encourage union organization in largely unorganized industries like steelmaking, meat-packing and auto production (see number 32, Rathborne).

The union movement during this period can be divided into two broad factions: radical and mainstream. Radical trade unions, most notably the Industrial Workers of the World (IWW), championed the use of extreme tactics like civil disobedience and sabotage (see number 33, Flynn). Mainstream unions sometimes joined in such efforts, like during the great postwar strike wave of 1919 (see number 34, O'Connor). However, the American Federation of Labor and its member unions tended to avoid strikes and support the government during times of crisis, including war and depression. Radicalism in the American labor movement proved short-lived. Government intervention in labor/management relations on the side of employers made it nearly impossible for unions that espoused radical ideas to function. The prosecution of IWW leaders during World War I for sedition is the best example of this phenomenon from this period. During the Depression, radical trade unions had a fantastic opportunity to grow because people were willing to consider such drastic measures in the face of economic catastrophe. Nevertheless, groups like the IWW and the American Communist Party played only a minor role in the labor disturbances of that period.

Nevertheless, when the Great Depression of the 1930s struck, many workers who had shown no previous evidence of militancy began to organize to improve their lives. An early example of such behavior is the activity of sharecroppers in the early 1930s (see number 36, Kester). More important to the entire American economy was the creation of the Committee (later Congress) of Industrial Organizations (CIO) in 1935. Unlike the American Federation of Labor (AFL), which only cared about organizing the best-paid, highest-skilled workers at this time, the CIO successfully organized unorganized workers (including many in traditionally nonunion industries) regardless of their skill level. In fact, the CIO was so successful that the AFL had to begin recruiting more less-skilled workers, despite previous philosophical objections to this strategy.

One of the tactics which CIO members pioneered was the sitdown strike (see number 37, Adamic). The most important sitdown strike in American history occurred at a Flint, Michigan, General Motors complex in 1937. This strike was largely responsible for trade unions entering the auto industry. Besides overcoming union opposition, the CIO's United Auto Workers also had to overcome opposition from AFL-affiliated workers., In fact, competition between the AFL and CIO hindered organizing efforts nationwide until the Federal government intervened to prevent labor disputes during World War II.

For working-class Americans of all kinds, culture served as a means to express unease at the perils of the American economy at this time. The tavern or saloon was one largely-male preserve for those with little else in their lives (see number 41, Mitchell).

Many such establishments offered not only camaraderie but job placement advice, even gambling and other illicit entertainment. When times got worse, culture became even more important to those workers who had little else. Farmers and their families fled the Dust Bowl in the Plains by the thousands. Like other workers, they often sang about their plight, (see number 38, Hunter). Many workers expressed the sentiment that they would rather help themselves than accept help from the government. Even a seemingly happy event like having one's wife get a high-paying war job could lead to anxiety in the man who once supported her (see number 40, Leadbelly). Victims of the Depression also took solace by telling their story to other workers in their same situation (see number 39, Morris).

In many ways, the period between the World Wars represented a time of unprecedented (and unequalled) power for the U.S. labor movement. The National Labor Relations Act and the Fair Labor Standards Act of 1937 (which, among other things, set the first federal minimum wage) form the cornerstone of American industrial relations to this day.

Work and Labor/
Management
Relations

*Serious accidents at steel mills, like the one shown here
at United States Steel's Gary Works, were often caused in part
by the long hours that workers labored, 1908.
Courtesy of Calumet Regional Archives,
Indiana University Northwest, Gary, Indiana.*

Mrs. L. L. Ray Outlines
Welfare Capitalism in a
New York Department Store, 1911

Answering the labor question was an all-consuming task for employ-
ers around the turn of the twentieth century, when they often found
themselves resorting to threats—and even violence—to keep employ-
ees in line. But after 1900, some firms showed an inclination to use
more carrot and less stick. Welfare capitalism (often called welfare
work at the time) refers to various measures employers took to see to
the personal welfare of their workers, even though their situation in
the labor market did not require them to do so. Employers hoped that
such benevolence would inspire gratitude in their workers, which in
turn would make them more productive. Some employers even saw
welfare capitalism as their personal duty toward their workforce.
Whatever the motivation, many industries adopted the practice dur-
ing this period.

Mrs. L. L. Ray was the Welfare Secretary for the Greenhut Siegel-
Cooper department store chain of New York City. Like many early
welfare capitalists, most of her employees were women. Here Ray
describes the welfare work at her firm to a meeting of the National
Civic Federation, a group of business and labor leaders who helped
spread welfare capitalism throughout the country.

I SHALL GIVE YOU a brief statement of what we do in department
stores. . . . We have a physician always in attendance and the
girls or men (and we have seven thousand employees in the two
stores, Greenhut's and Siegel-Cooper's) may consult this doctor

Excerpt from Mrs. L. L. Ray, "The Department Store Problem," Eleventh
Annual Meeting, The National Civic Federation (New York: J. J. Little & Ives
Co., 1911), 378–80.

any day of the year. All of the medicines are free and they receive half of their salary when ill for six weeks in one year. Of course, that is extended if I investigate and find it necessary. . . .

In regard to the welfare manager, we have a complete office where different employees can come and bring various complaints. The disposition of the case is left entirely to the manager. If it is very important and involves several problems, I can consult Mr. Greenhut or any manager at any time. I can get access when others could not; otherwise the solution of a problem would linger and nothing would be accomplished. It is the greatest pleasure to work with the people—all cooperate so beautifully. I have not been refused one thing asked as yet. Through consultation, we have secured a better sick room. It had been an eyesore and was not large enough. I have had supplemented a recreation room, rest room and reading room combined, way at the top of the house —a sun parlor. The girls use the roof for recreation, the boys take walks and the men smoke. They seem to object to having a smoking room and say they would rather get out. We have a lunch room, where food is served to employees for less than cost. The milk is examined and the food inspected, and we are always glad to have others come and test it. I was very glad to hear the gentleman who talked on ventilation. I have used in the windows copper wire. In that way, we have ventilation and no one can see into the rooms; there is privacy and the girls and men feel better about it. This welfare work is beautiful. It is like an endless chain. I do not see how we could do without it. One can readily see that with 7,000 employes, there is a field for thought and a great deal to be done. The welfare department is helping the needy; it lessens the work of charity organizations, because we take care of our vast family as far as we can. We have to refer some to the Charity Organization Society and I am glad to say they cooperate with me. At any time that I can give positions to their people who are worthy, I am glad to help them in that way. When it is necessary to investigate a sick case—where we have been interested in a particular girl or man—and get into the home and see the environment, then we know the why and the wherefore—[we can] understand better how to handle cases. We see the parents and what the girls are accustomed to and what she has not had and we can work so much better. That to me is one of the best things we do. We get in personal contact and gain the confidence of the employes. They come to us with their troubles. If there is some domestic trouble they come and ask advice about it and it is surprising how we can help them. Mr. Greenhut's motto is always help them to help themselves.

How can you best help them? Go to their homes and see the problems bearing on the case; don't let it rest until tomorrow; do it then and there; that is the best way I think, and then go on to the next. If you go to the home you will find possibly a father out of work or a sister home sick and all the burden falling on the girl. Then, we must ask some help to lift that burden. In many cases it requires hospital treatment. Where she lives in a furnished room and a girl has no way of supplying personal needs, there being objections even to a cup of coffee, that I call a hospital case at once and notify a physician. He says call a carriage or an ambulance and takes the girl to the hospital. I visit them and see that they are properly cared for—never lose sight of the cases and we get a little nearer all the time. I think we do get nearer to anyone when they are afflicted and want help and love. The principal thing needed is sympathy. We always have to stay above to pull a man out of the mud and must see from their point of view as well as our own; give them that love that the whole world is eager for and let them see that people are interested in them and then use, of course, the greatest amount of tact. You cannot handle two cases alike; what will do for one will not do for the other.

We need more welfare workers. I am glad to be associated with them, meet them and see the beautiful things they have done.

Questions

1. Why do you think Greenhut Siegel-Cooper employed Mrs. Ray? Was it more for the good of its employees or for the good of its business?
2. Why do you think Mrs. Ray concentrated her speech on women employees rather than on then men who worked at her firm?
3. Do you think the employees had as good an opinion of Greenhut Siegel-Cooper's welfare work as Mrs. Ray did? Why or why not?

Whiting Williams Endures Long Hours Working in a Steel Mill, 1921

With the advent of industrialization, American workers increasingly endured long shifts, sometimes twelve to fourteen hours per day, or risked losing their jobs. Indeed, those workers unwilling to accept such long workdays were easily replaced by other desperate workers. There-fore, for much of the late-nineteenth century, many workers cared more about gaining shorter hours than gaining higher wages.

In the steel industry, the twelve-hour day became commonplace during the 1880s, about the same time that managers eliminated unions from the steel trade. Although many industries abandoned the twelve-hour day after World War I, it continued in the steel indus-try until 1923 because industry executives believed that giving it up would prove to be too costly. Whiting Williams, a personnel director at a specialty steel company, gave up his position to understand work from labor's point of view. Here, in a book he wrote about his experi-ence, he describes what it was like to work the twelve-hour day at an unnamed steel mill.

Excerpt from Whiting Williams, *What's on the Worker's Minds* (New York: Charles Scribner's Sons, 1921), 18–21.

Stackton,*
Wednesday, February 12.

Well, I will say that the ten-hour day turn is enormously easier than the twelve-hour night shift. But when begun Monday morning immediately after a week of night work totaling eighty-seven hours—we did seventeen hours up to Sunday noon—it is not particularly conducive to an enthusiastic picture of life in general. A hot bath and clean clothes, after taking off unbelievably dirty and sweaty working togs, and shaking them out of the window (shovelling up soot at the bottom of a hot, drafty chimney is *hot and dirty!*) does marvels to set you up sufficiently to eat supper ravenously. But shortly after that you again feel as though it might be well to go to bed to get ready for more labor—or else try a movie or some other form of passing time removed as far as possible from both mental and physical effort.

If this town were asked to put its views into words it would ponder hardly a moment before condensing it into three words—*"What the hell?"* From top to bottom that seems the general formula and prescription. It is, I'm sure, only the result, or at least the symptom, of the general overwork.

The gang bosses, at least those of the labor gangs, seem to be the worst examples of the what-the-hell philosophy. Of course no question is, apparently, ever asked regarding any matter whatsoever in the plant except in the name of the Devil's abode. But our bosses can put into it an amount of heat and steam which makes it really terrifying to the tired worker who perhaps took ten or fifteen more minutes than positively necessary to "catch-drink-water"—as these bosses would say in their broken English—or who sat down because no boss gave him any orders at the moment. But, "what-the-hell" can come from anything whatever—very often from the foreman's own failure to give proper instructions.

"T'row bricks offa track—over dere!"

Everybody throws bricks in the general direction of boss's fingers.

---

*Stackton is the pseudonym that Williams gives the town where the steel mill he worked at was located.

Fifteen minutes later, boss returns—

"What da hell! Why you t'row bricks over damn ventilator? No can work furnace. Me tell you t'row bricks over dere."

I presume the bosses are quite as tired as the rest of the crowd because they spend just as many hours in the plant as we do—though they seldom touch shovel, bar, or brick—and are supposed to worry about 'getting the job done. Which last is the *very last* thing any of us under them ever worry about—unless it's an especially easy job, when whispers go 'round—"Dees fine job— take easy—mebbe make last all day."

But don't get the idea that the average labor boss really does any head work—or lets anybody else do it.

To-day six or eight of us were taking the very heavy checker-brick out of one of the checker-chambers, or large rooms under the "floor" of the furnaces, and so on a level with the cinder-pit. Here the bricks are laid at right angles to each other with square air spaces in between like checkerboards. The great roomful of square-set fire-brick thus serves to catch and retain the heat from the air and smoke passing through it from the furnace on the way to the stack in order to give it back to the cold air from outside which enters the furnace during every alternate half-hour or so when the draft is reversed by the first or second helpers in charge—that alternate direction of the draft through alternate sets of the "checkers" enables the "regenerating furnace" to keep getting hotter and hotter till the "charge" of metals is melted, the carbon brought to the right proportion, and the steel is made. Another dozen or more of us were tossing these bricks from man to man till they were piled up high against the wall of the building—the soot having dropped off them meanwhile. At the same time an Indian (from Mexico) high up on practically the same pile, was tossing them down via an equally long line of men into the next checker-chamber of the same furnace. When I diplomatically suggested that the piling up seemed unnecessary, the answer of course was, "What the hell!" Later the piling was stopped, and a great long line of about ten men pitched brick from one to another needlessly for a distance of thirty feet till I lost my temper and the boss finally arranged a line of about ten feet, whereby the bricks came from one chamber and went back into the other— with a saving of about eight men's time.

The men, of course, get to feeling that their work is never done. They have not the slightest interest in what it means or how it affects the operations of the mill around them because, I *will* say, nobody tries very hard to give it to them. It is all just a matter of doing as little work as the boss will allow.

Last week I tried to get the good notice of the different overseers by sticking close to my knitting. The bunch, of course, discouraged it—"What the hell! Lotsa time" and the bosses noticed me only when, after a long turn of work, I rested a moment. Their notice was the usual "Hey, dere! What da hell! Do you t'ink dis sleeping place?"

Not always is this query put in a mean way. But it simply expresses complete lack of effort to secure interest or to give instruction. The only thing in the world these "boys" have to give, or are asked to give, is their physical strength. They are hardly to be blamed if they try to guard their only capital by as many breathing-spells and as slow motions as the boss will stand for.

Here's an example in "physical arithmetic":

From Monday evening to Monday evening, on night turn, a man here works eighty-seven out of the week's one hundred and sixty-eight hours. Of the remaining eighty-one he sleeps, at seven hours a day, a total of forty-nine; eats not over ten; walks or travels in a street-car, say, ten; dresses, shaves, tends furnace, undresses, winds alarm clock and gets occasional drink, say eight. What does he think the rest of the time—during all those remaining four hours!

To save turning over to the end of the book, I'll slip anybody the answer: *"What the hell!"*

QUESTIONS

1. Why would any worker accept a job that required twelve hours of labor a day?
2. If the twelve-hour day encouraged employees to loaf, why didn't the steel industry implement shorter hours sooner?
3. Was adopting a "What-the-Hell?" attitude a form of rebellion? Why or why not?

30

Paul Taylor on the "American-Mexican Frontier"

In the early twentieth century, Texas ranchers began to bring large numbers of Mexicans across the border to harvest crops. People of Mexican descent in Texas proper had done this work for generations, but, just as industrialists manipulated European immigrants into working more cheaply and dangerously than native-born Americans, Texas agriculturalists applied the same logic to Mexican immigrants.

University of California sociologist Paul Schuster Taylor devoted much of his career to investigating the conditions of America's poorest workers. Like his wife, photographer Dorothea Lange, Taylor believed that most Americans had no idea how widespread severe poverty was in the United States. Lange and Taylor believed that their work in art and academia would raise public awareness of the plight of their subjects and perhaps improve their chances to raise the quality of their lives.

"WET" MEXICANS, i.e., those illegally in the United States, according to an American farmer were "at a disadvantage in bargaining. One farmer reported his Mexican tenant to the immigration service to get his crop." Mexicans, too, were acutely conscious of the the disabilities of the "wets."

Greater advantages were taken of the "wets" closer to the Rio Grande. On December 10, 1928, near Mission, Texas, a Mexican replied to my inquiry concerning wages: "Farm wages are $1 to $1.25 and $1.50 to $1.75 [depending on the season and crop] if

From *An American-Mexican Frontier* by Paul S. Taylor. Copyright © 1934 by the University of North Carolina Press, pp. 138–141. Used by permission of the publisher.

you have your [immigration] papers. If you don't have papers, wages are 50 cents or whatever you can get."

An interesting phase of labor relations is the hostility of competitors that prevailed between white, Negro and Mexican laborers, characterizing particularly the feelings of the two former toward the latter, who almost monopolized employment. White laborers stated that they had found it difficult to secure employment at various times because of Mexican competition both in Nueces County and in north Texas, and had been frankly told that this was the reason.

The lower living standards of Mexicans were felt to be a menace; for, as one American said, "I can't live on hot tamales and green peppers and my family ain't going to, if I have to go out and steal it. We *have* lived on $1 a day, but we didn't have the necessaries of life. I am going to have white man's food." Although statements were generally made that Mexicans worked cheaper, as to cotton picking, a white picker said, "It's mainly the wets who work for less; after they've been here a while they want more money." A Mexican farmer himself complained that "A lot of fellows just from over there go to work and don't ask what the wages are." The accusation by a Negro cotton picker was particularly interesting because of his almost immediate and utterly unconscious contradiction of his main charge:

> The Mexicans will work cheaper and keep the prices down. They can live on next to nothing. A *tortilla* and a cup of coffee will stand them for a day. We eat meat and bread about the same as you-all. Yes, we could work on less but we don't want to. . . There used to be Mexicans here on this farm but they moved away. Why? They wanted $1.25 for picking. We pick for $1; it was good cotton.

With cotton of varying degrees of attractiveness, and a large and mobile labor supply, undoubtedly under-cutting of this sort was likely to be done by almost anyone; no one, however, made such charges against white laborers, although Negroes and Mexicans made them against each other, and Americans said that they both worked cheaper than whites. Inability to mix whites, Negroes, and Mexicans at work was asserted by a farmer, because "each thinks he's superior." The charge was most frequently made as a reason for not employing white cotton pickers, and referred usually to associations after working hours. Negroes and Mexicans worked together on the track at times, but generally, the three groups were kept separate when picking cotton.

. . .

The mobility of Mexican labor during the picking season has often disturbed the farmers, who usually wish their pickers to remain until after the harvest is completed. Sometimes, however, other farmers induce their neighbors' hands to leave, by offering either a higher price, or better picking. In either case, but especially the former, there was strong resistance to the practice of "stealing labor." In 1918 a representative of the County Council of Defense, District War Council of the County, declared,

> . . . you shall inform the farmers of your community that efforts and schemes on the part of farmers to get labor away from their neighbors by offering them higher prices or other inducements, will not be tolerated by this organization. You will let it be known in your community that such underhanded action on the part of any person will be considered as an unpatriotic and disloyal act.

Again, in 1920 a speaker at a farmers' meeting inveighed against the practice of "labor theft" by a farmer who made no effort to get pickers into the county, and who lured away the hands transported by his neighbor by offering a premium.

"I had rather a man come to my corn crib in the night and steal my corn than to have them bid my pickers away from me," he said amid applause. He declared the belief that the majority of the people stood for the right and expressed the opinion that there should be a committee whose duty it should be to call on men making a practice of hiring their neighbor's help away, and "make 'em behave."

QUESTIONS

1. In what ways did Mexican workers exercise power against the farmers who employed them?
2. What were the sources of conflict between workers of different racial and ethnic backgrounds?
3. If you were a union organizer in southern Texas in the late 1920s, how would you go about organizing cotton pickers?

31
Evelyn Gotzion Recalls Factory Work during World War II

During World War II, American women entered the workforce in record numbers, replacing men who left their jobs to serve in the armed forces. Most of these women needed no prompting. Not only was it patriotic to serve one's country, but high-paying war jobs had great appeal to workers who had just lived through the Depression. Yet such jobs had their bad points, too.

Evelyn Gotzion worked at Rayovac, a battery company based in Madison, Wisconsin, from 1935 until 1978. During those years, she raised three children in a two-income family. In this oral history, part of a series of interviews with women recounting their lives during wartime, Gotzion discusses the accelerated nature of factory work during World War II. She goes on to describe how shop-floor problems and rank-and-file solutions to them propelled her into union activity. Thanks to her experience, Gotzion remained a union activist throughout her career.

I HAD ALL KINDS of jobs. Then we had one line, a big line, where when you'd work ten hours and you'd stand in one spot or sit in one spot. It got terrible, all day long. So I suggested to my foreman, the general foreman, that we take turns of learning everybody's job and switching every half hour. Well, they didn't like it, but we were on the side, every once in a while, learning each other's job and learning how to do it, so eventually most all

Excerpt from the recollections of Evelyn Gotzion, in Michael E. Stevens and Ellen D. Goldlust, eds. *Women Remember the War, 1941-1945* (Madison, State Historical Society of Wisconsin Press, 1993), 26–29. Text reprinted with permission of the Wisconsin Historical Society.

of us got so we could do all the jobs, [of] which there were probably fifteen or twenty on the line. We could do every job so we
could go up and down the line and rotate. And then they found
out that that was really a pretty good thing to do because it made
the people happier, and they could take each other's place when
they had to go to the bathroom. There wasn't that many extra
people to get around there if you had to go into the nurse or
something to take your place. And the foremen were so busy,
they couldn't come. And then we had government inspectors that
walked around there and checked everything we did.

So it worked out real great, but we had a lot of problems
trying to consent to letting them do it. I know this one day, this
one lady and I had changed jobs and my boss said, "What are you
doing down in this position?" I said, "I am doing her job, and
she's doing mine." I said, "If you don't think I can do it right, the
government inspector was just here, Ed was just here, he said
I'm doing fine." My inspector was here now. I said, "Why don't
you stand here, too, and then when you get done with me, you go
up and see her."

[Interviewer asks:] Did the union help convince management
to allow you to switch jobs?

No, no. This was just my idea because we got so tired of
standing in one spot. But then one day I was the steward, and
they wouldn't listen to me. They cut our rates, so I shut off the
line, and the boss came up and he said, "What are you doing?" I
said, "Well, I have asked everybody that I know why we have
gotten a cut in pay and why we're doing exactly the same amount
of work as we did. The only thing you did was change your box
down there and you open it from another end. That's all I can see
that's different. I went up and down the line, I've talked to everybody. There's nothing different. How can you change our job?"
[He said,] "Well, you turn that line on, or I'm going to send you
into the office." I said, "I wish you'd send me into the office."
"Well," he said, "You turn the line on and I'll get somebody down
here to talk to." So the rate setter came down and I said, "Would
you please explain it and write it out on a piece of paper, because
all the people on this line are real interested to know what's going on." He said, "No, I have a right to set the rate the way I want

to and I see how it's done." I think [that] when we all could do each other's job and they found it out efficiently, they maybe thought it was too easy for us or something.

So, anyhow, we wrote up a big grievance and they all signed it and then I called the president of the union and then we had a meeting and then we had the other stewards in on it. Then we called our Milwaukee office and they sent a man in, and they said they thought we had a good grievance, and so then we had a meeting with the management and at that point the president decided that I should be added to the bargaining committee so that I would go in and argue our case, because I could do it better than any of the rest of them because I knew what it was. So I went along in to the management with the union.

First of all, they wanted to know what I was doing there. I was not a union executive. [I was no] more than a steward, and when had we changed our policy, and then they went on to tell them what had happened. We argued it, [and] then they brought in another guy from someplace else, the company did, and then we did. We finally got it straightened out, and we got our back pay, too. From then on I was on the bargaining committee all the years that I worked at Rayovac. I was never voted off the committee because if I thought there was something right I wasn't afraid to argue for it and fight for it. I didn't care whose toes I stepped on, really. If it was right, it was right. Well, management wasn't very kind to me for a while. But when there was something to do in the plant like solicit for United Givers and all of that, they always asked me to do it. I guess I didn't hurt myself too much. At least I felt better because I knew it was right and we had two or three real older ladies, lot older than me, working on that line and they worked hard and I knew they were dragging when night come, they were so tired out, and I thought, "Why should they work for less money? The government is paying the company all this money and they're getting it all. Why aren't we getting some of it? We should get something, too."

QUESTIONS

1. To what extent would Gotzion's story have been different if she were a man? How did her concerns transcend gender differences?
2. Why didn't the union initially respond to the concerns of Gotzion and her fellow line-workers?
3. How did federal government oversight during the war affect Gotzion's story of workers' solutions to their problems?

32

Mervyn Rathborne Testifies in Defense of the National Labor Relations Act, 1939

In 1933, Congress passed and President Roosevelt signed the National Industrial Recovery Act (NIRA). Section 7(a) of that act recognized the right of American workers to join unions and bargain collectively with their employers for the first time. Although the Supreme Court declared the NIRA unconstitutional in 1935, Congress and the president quickly approved the National Labor Relations Act (NLRA, sometimes called the Wagner Act after its author, Senator Robert Wagner of New York) to take its place. The Supreme Court declared the NLRA constitutional in 1937.

The NLRA again guaranteed workers' rights to join unions and bargain collectively. It also created the National Labor Relations Board to enforce a series of rules regarding collective bargaining that applied to both labor and management.

In the first years of the Wagner Act, both union membership and strike activity in the United States exploded. Employers and conservative unions, looking for a way to stem this tide, proposed a series of unsuccessful amendments to the NLRA in 1939. Here, Mervyn Rathborne, president of the American Communications Association, defends the act before a congressional committee considering these amendments. Not only his union, but the whole Congress of Industrial Organizations (CIO) to which his union belonged, as well as the American Federation of Labor (from which the CIO split), had made great strides in organization since the NLRA's passage. However, Rathborne defends the act not just in self-interested terms, but by pointing out what NLRA-induced collective bargaining could do for all nonunionized workers.

Excerpt from the United States Senate Committee on Education and Labor, "National Labor Relations Act and Proposed Amendments," Part 20, 76th Congress, 1st session, July 26 and 31, 1939, 3883–84.

THE PREAMBLE of the National Labor Relations Act declares:

> It is hereby declared to be the policy of the United States to elimi-
> nate certain substantial obstructions to the free flow of commerce
> and to mitigate and eliminate these obstructions when they have
> occurred by encouraging the practice and procedure of collective
> bargaining and by protecting the exercises by workers of full free-
> dom, association, and self-organization and designation of repre-
> sentatives of their own choosing for the purpose of negotiating the
> terms and conditions of their employ, or other mutual aid or pro-
> tection.

The record clearly indicates that the National Labor Relations Act has encouraged collective bargaining. In 1935 the membership of the American Federation of Labor was approximately
3,000,000. Today the combined membership of the A. F. of L. and
the C. I. O. is approximately 8,000,000.

I believe that the act has done much more than merely encourage collective bargaining. It has freed hundreds of thousands
of the working men and women of America from a type of economic bondage which has prevented them, in many cases, from
exercising the political rights guaranteed by the Constitution of
the United States.

Our experience has shown that the lack of effective trade-
union organization, and employer domination or control of many
existing unions, has permitted employers to create a condition of
economic bondage which prevents thousands of American workers from fully exercising their rights as citizens.

An examination of the conditions of the sharecroppers in
the South, the coal miners in Harlan County, Ky., the agricultural workers in California, and other oppressed groups of industrial and agricultural workers should prove this contention.

The substandard economic conditions of these groups have
drastically limited their participation in and contribution to the
social, cultural, and political life of our country.

The National Labor Relations Act has given these economically enslaved workers a new freedom.

To the extent that it has promoted this new freedom, the
National Labor Relations Act has strengthened our democratic
institutions. It is fundamental to the American philosophy of

government, I believe, that the denial to any citizen of the rights guaranteed by the Constitution weakens democracy, while conversely, democracy is strengthened by the extension of these rights to citizens who previously have not been able to exercise them freely.

Despite the adoption of a policy by the United States to encourage "the peace and procedure of collective bargaining," there has not been a general acceptance of collective bargaining by the employers of this country. This is clearly reflected in the figures on the number of organized workers in America as compared to other democratic countries. According to a report of the National Industrial Conference Board for May 1939, there are approximately 37,000,000 employed and unemployed industrial and agricultural wage earners in this country; of this number about 8,000,000 are members of trade unions. From these figures we can conclude that about 21 percent of the industrial and agricultural workforce enjoy the benefits of collective bargaining. A report of a special commission appointed by President Roosevelt in 1938 to study labor conditions in Great Britain and the Scandinavian countries shows that employers in these countries have accepted collective bargaining to a much greater degree than those in the United States. In its report the Commission stated that in June 1938 the National Federation of the Swedish Trade Unions included 42 trade-union federations, with 7,135 local unions, having a total membership of about 850,000 workers. This membership represents approximately 65 percent of all manual workers in Sweden. Compare this with the data on the state of labor organization in America. Therefore it is suggested that the committee, in its examination of amendments to the act, give consideration as to whether the administration of the act has been effective in encouraging the practice and procedure of collective bargaining and whether those who now propose amendments to the act are not, in fact, attempting by devious methods to completely abolish collective bargaining.

It is our belief that many of the groups who are seeking to emasculate the act through amendment are doing so because they don't want to obey the law, and many of these groups are people who have refused to obey the law while it has been in force, and

I think that it should be clear that those people are opposed to collective bargaining as such, and they are merely bringing forward these amendments because they do not feel they can get the complete repeal of the act. . . .

We are firm in the opinion that the National Labor Relations Act and its administration have brought many benefits to millions of American workers in both the A. F. of L. and C. I. O. Therefore, despite the fact that our union has received rough treatment at the hands of the [National Labor Relations] Board* on several occasions, we are opposed to any amendment to the act or any change in the personnel of the Board.

QUESTIONS

1. Why does Rathborne contend that union representation is necessary for Americans to exercise the full rights of citizenship? What is the relationship between economic status and political rights?
2. Why might American employers have been more opposed to unions than those in other countries? Is this still true today?
3. Some people contend that unions are no longer necessary in today's economy. Would a proposal to eliminate the National Labor Relations Act entirely find support today? Should such a proposal be enacted?

*The National Labor Relations Board (NLRB) is the government body established by the National Labor Relations Act to carry out and enforce the law's provisions.

The Union
Movement

Sitdown strikers in the Fisher body plant factory number three. Flint, Michigan, 1937. The great Flint Sitdown strike was the most important of many sitdown strikes to occur during the middle-late 1930s. Courtesy of the Library of Congress. # LC-USZ62-131617 DLC

33

Elizabeth Gurley Flynn Justifies Sabotage, 1916

Elizabeth Gurley Flynn was one of the founding members of the In-
dustrial Workers of the World. Her nickname, "The Rebel Girl," was a
sign of the important role she played in IWW actions throughout the
United States in the years leading up to World War I.

The IWW primarily organized among the most exploited work-
ers in the country such as the immigrant mill workers of Massachu-
setts or the primarily Mexican copper miners of Arizona. The ob-
stacles of working with such powerless constituencies prompted the
Wobblies to develop a series of strategies which most unions never
even considered. In this excerpt from an official IWW pamphlet she
wrote, Flynn explains why sabotaging the means of production is the
logical extension of more conventional labor struggles.

I AM NOT GOING to attempt to justify, sabotage on any moral ground.
If the workers consider that sabotage is necessary, that in itself
makes sabotage moral. Its necessity is its excuse for existence.
And for us to discuss the morality of sabotage would be as absurd
as to discuss the morality of the strike or the morality of the class
struggle itself. In order to understand sabotage or to accept it at
all it is necessary to accept the concept of the class struggle. If
you believe that between the workers on the one side and their
employers on the other there is peace, there is harmony such as
exists between brothers, and that consequently whatever strikes
and lockouts occur are simply family squabbles; if you believe

Excerpt from Elizabeth Gurley Flynn, "Sabotage: The Conscious Withdrawal
of the Workers' Industrial Efficiency" (Cleveland: I.W.W. Publishing Bureau,
October, 1916), 2–5.

that a point can be reached whereby the employer can get enough and the worker can get enough, a point of amicable adjustment of industrial warfare and economic distribution, then there is no justification and no explanation of sabotage intelligible to you. Sabotage is one weapon in the arsenal of labor to fight its side of the class struggle. Labor realizes, as it becomes more intelligent, that it must have power in order to accomplish anything; that neither appeals for sympathy nor abstract rights will make for better conditions. For instance, take an industrial establishment such as a silk mill, where men and women and little children work ten hours a day for an average wage of between six and seven dollars a week. Could any one of them, or a committee representing the whole, hope to induce the employer to give better conditions by appealing to his sympathy, by telling him of the misery, the hardship and the poverty of their lives; or could they do it by appealing to his sense of justice? Suppose that an individual working man or woman went to an employer and said, "I make, in my capacity as wage worker in this factory, so many dollars' worth of wealth every day and justice demands that you give me at least half." The employer would probably have him removed to the nearest lunatic asylum. He would consider him too dangerous a criminal to let loose on the community! It is neither sympathy nor justice that makes an appeal to the employer. But it is power. If a committee can go to the employer with this ultimatum: "We represent all the men and women in this shop. They are organized in a union as you are organized in a manufacturers' association. They have met and formulated in that union a demand for better hours and wages and they are not going to work one day longer unless they get it. In other words, they have withdrawn their power as wealth producers from your plant and they are going to coerce you by this withdrawal of their power; into granting their demands," that sort of ultimatum served upon an employer usually meets with an entirely different response; and if the union is strongly enough organized and they are able to make good their threat they usually accomplish what tears and pleadings never could have accomplished.

We believe that the class struggle existing in society is expressed in the economic power of the master on the one side and the growing economic power of the workers on the other side meeting in open battle now and again, but meeting in continual daily conflict over which shall have the larger share of labor's product and the ultimate ownership of the means of life. The employer wants long hours, the intelligent workingman wants short hours. The employer wants low wages, the intelligent workingman wants high wages. The employer is not concerned with the sanitary conditions in the mill, he is concerned only with keeping the cost of production at a minimum; the intelligent workingman is concerned, cost or no cost, with having ventilation, sanitation and lighting that will be conducive to his physical welfare. Sabotage is to this class struggle what the guerrilla warfare is to the battle. The strike is the open battle of the class struggle, sabotage is the guerrilla warfare, the day-by-day warfare between two opposing classes. . . .

. . . Sabotage means primarily: *the withdrawal of efficiency.* Sabotage means either to slacken up and interfere with the quantity, or to botch in your skill and interfere with the quality, of capitalist production or to give poor service. Sabotage is not physical violence, sabotage is an internal, industrial process. It is something that is fought out within the four walls of the shop. And these three forms of sabotage—to affect the quality, the quantity and the service are aimed at affecting the profit of the employer. Sabotage is a means of striking at the employer's profit for the purpose of forcing him into granting certain conditions, even as workingmen strike for the same purpose of coercing him. It is simply another form of coercion.

QUESTIONS

1. Can sabotage ever be justified on moral grounds? Explain.
2. Is Flynn correct with regard to how management might respond to a single worker's call for justice?
3. Are sabotage and strikes different methods of fighting the same war?

Harvey O'Connor
Remembers the Seattle General Strike, 1919

In most strikes, members of one union go on strike at one work place. But in a general strike, every union in any industry in a particular area—usually a city—strikes for the same purpose. The Seattle General Strike of 1919, coming as it did just two years after the Communist (Bolshevik) Revolution in Russia and during a year in which the United States experienced many other labor strikes, is particularly important as a sign of postwar labor militancy and because of the fierce backlash it generated in the press and big business.

The strike started in support of Seattle shipyard workers who were fighting to maintain wage gains they had achieved during World War I. The Seattle Labor Council, an umbrella organization that included nearly every trade union in the city, did not want to let the economy collapse. To avoid harm to working people in or outside unions, it maintained kitchens where workers could get meals. It also organized essential city services (like laundry service for hospitals) so that the city could continue to function despite the strike. The labor journalist Harvey O'Connor was a young man during the strike. In a memoir written in his old age, he describes the effect of the strike on the city and some of the fierce backlash by reactionary forces that brought it to an end in just five days.

PEOPLE—STAYED HOME. The *New York Tribune*'s correspondent, sent out at some expense to cover a revolution, reported that "there was absolutely no violence. The normal police docket of a hundred a day fell to about 30." [Seattle] Mayor [Ole] Hanson had sworn in 600 extra police and deputized 2,400 more at a cost to

Excerpt from Harvey O'Connor, *Revolution in Seattle*, 138–45. Copyright © 1964 by Monthly Review Press. Reprinted by permission of Monthly Review Foundation.

the city of $50,000. But the commanding general of the U.S. troops brought into the city said he had never seen such a quiet and orderly city. The *Star* managed to get out a bobtailed edition with the few printers working, distributed free from trucks manned by police with machine guns. It was headed, in red ink, SEATTLE, UNITED STATES OF AMERICA, across the top of the page. It boasted that clubs, revolvers, rifles, carbines, automatics, and machine guns were being distributed among the fearful. It reported that trucks, sandbagged and with machine guns able to sweep the streets, were lumbering up and down the main avenues of the city. But there was nobody there to shoot down. Rumors spread fast. The strikers had dynamited the city's water supply dam, Ole Hanson had been assassinated, buildings were being blown up and troops were engaged in bloody battles with strikers on down-town streets. In all this Mayor Hanson was hardly a help. To eager newspaper correspondents he was already proclaiming that he had quelled, almost single-handed, an attempted Bolshevik revolution. Newspapers in the East greedily gulped down such news, as the nation gaped with bated breath for the outcome of this killer-diller thriller. Hanson telephoned Secretary Duncan [of the strike Committee] to demand that the strike be ended forthwith. Although he refused "to treat with these revolutionists" in statements he gave the wire services, he invited the Committee of 15 to City Hall and promised if the strike were ended that he personally would go to Washington to plead the shipyard workers' case. If not, he would call out the army and declare martial law—a prerogative beyond his power.

The *P-I* [the *Seattle Post-Intelligencer* newspaper] in a front page editorial thundered: "The issue is no longer in doubt; the leaders of the revolt are openly proclaiming that the shipyard strike is only a pretext; that it is a camouflage. It is not a strike; it is a delirium-born rebellion." The *Star* chimed in: "A part of our community is, in fact, defying our government and is, in fact, contemplating changing that government, and not by *American Methods*. This small part of our city talks plainly of 'taking over things,' of 'resuming under our own management.'"

In the meantime the strike machinery was working a lot more efficiently than the most hopeful had expected. Thirty-five milk stations were functioning in the residential sections; 21 cafeterias were serving meals for 25 cents apiece to union men, for 35 cents to others; hospitals were getting their linen and fuel. A union card was the only credential for the 25-cent meal, and an I.W.W. card was as good as an A.F. of L. The Japanese Labor Association, comprising hotel and restaurant workers, struck in sympathy with the labor movement which had never recognized them nor even regarded them as a part of unionism. The I.W.W. saw to it that the ginmills on the skid road were shut down (Washington had had official prohibition since 1916) and that I.W.W. members kept off the streets.

The exhilaration from the marvellous display of solidarity experienced Thursday and Friday began by Saturday to give way to apprehension. The purpose of the strike was to help the ship-yard workers get an honorable settlement of their demands. But nobody on the other side seemed inclined to negotiate anything. While Mayor Hanson's fulminations helped to keep up the backs of unionists, the ominous silence in Washington was dismaying. It had been assumed that the general strike would shock officialdom into action and negotiation. No one had questioned that the government would insist on settlement of some kind. It was assumed that ships were needed, and the government would come to terms. But the war was over and while more shipping was needed to replace the tonnage sunk by German submarines, there was no longer any great urgency about it. The shipyards along the East and Gulf Coasts and in California continued oper-ating. The truth was that Seattle was expendable, despite its record-breaking speed in delivering ships. For all Washington cared, the Seattle yards could remain closed; moreover it was desirable that the unions be taught a lesson. The P-I observed that "the big fact that stands out from the temporary confusion of business is that Seattle, given a brief time for readjustment, would be well off, if not better than before, if the whole of its striking population were suddenly withdrawn from the city."

That the shipyards were expendable was apparent enough to the Citizens Committee, headed by a distinguished divine and an eminent banker. The Committee of 15 was informed that be-cause the strike was considered a revolutionary attempt, it would not bargain on surrender terms. Call off the strike, and then, per-haps. . . .

From the Citizens Committee Mayor Hanson got his cue. Friday evening he ordered the Committee of 15 to end the strike Saturday morning, or else. His "or else" was an empty threat but it had the effect of stiffening opposition among unionists to yielding to such pressure.

Far more effective were the threats of international union officials to revoke local union charters, particularly in the printing trades. Small editions of the dailies began to appear. On Saturday a few unions returned to work; that afternoon the Committee of 15 voted 13 to 1 to end the strike at midnight. Although several more unions had voted the same day to return, the General Strike Committee, with final authority, voted to continue the strike by 76 to 45. In late afternoon it had seemed that the vote to end the strike was assured; but after a dinner recess several unions changed their position upon the urging of the metal trades and longshore unions.

The General Strike Committee met again Monday morning and then adopted the motion to end the strike. More unions had gone back to work, but others which had returned Saturday voted to resume the strike and bring it to an end with united tanks at noon Tuesday, February 11. The strike had lasted five working days.

For the majority of Seattle unions, there was no sense of defeat as the strike ended. They had demonstrated their solidarity with their brothers in the yards, and the memory of the great days when labor had shown its strength glowed in their minds. It was not until many years later, in a very different climate of opinion, that some of the leaders began apologizing for what could be excused as a momentary aberration by an otherwise solid body of citizenry. It became needful to rewrite history, to blame the general strike on "radicals" or "the I.W.W. element." Forgetful of the evident fact that the strike was voted by some 300 delegates chosen for the purpose from a hundred local unions, almost unanimously, and that none but these regular delegates and their Committee of 15 made the decisions, some have apologized for the great general strike of Seattle as merely an incident to be forgotten, glossed over, or explained away.

The Central Labor Council resumed its normal position in the movement on Wednesday, February 12, the day after the strike ended. Delegates reviewed the impressive achievements of the committees which had carried out the tasks assigned them in guarding against violence, in feeding the hungry, caring for the sick, and keeping essential services running. Chairman Ben F. Nauman of the strike committee summed up: "We did something in this strike which has never been done before by the A.F. of L. We pulled off a general strike with craft unions, with ironclad contracts which had to be broken, and with a constitution that had to be ignored." There had been two mistakes, he said: the failure to decide on the duration of the strike at the beginning, and the failure to call it off Saturday night when it became evident that the ranks were breaking. . . .

Seattleites read with some astonishment the lurid accounts of the general strike which appeared in the nation's leading magazines. To the *Saturday Evening Post* it was evident that "bolshevism has put forth its supremest effort in America and has failed." There followed a curious tale, typical of that hysterical period. "The I.W.W. themselves," said the *Post*, "openly boast that the Russian revolution was planned in the office of a Seattle lawyer, counsel for the organization, during those three over-heated days wherein Lenin and Trotsky tarried in the city's midst, en route to Russia; and that an American revolution was planned or at least discussed at the same time." The *Post* referred to "an especially illuminating little treatise in booklet form entitled *Russia Did It*, by an ambitious young Bolshevik author who, alas, now languishes behind prison bars in lieu of $10,000 bail. Two and a half tons of this booklet alone were distributed. Equity [the socialist-I.W.W. print shop] ran its presses frantically day and night." Alas, too, for the truth: it wasn't a booklet but a rather small leaflet; the "Bolshevik author" far from languishing in jail was working to help Armour's construct a huge agricultural irrigation project in the Sutter Basin of California; the leaflet was issued in a modest quantity of 20,000 amounting only to several pounds weight in all; and Equity managed to get its work done in one eight-hour shift each day.

World's Work, then a leading national magazine, was not to be outdone by the *Post*. A full-page photo of Mayor Hanson was captioned:

156 PART III: 1914–1945

> A citizen of Norwegian ancestry who, by a quick display of intelligent energy, crushed in a few hours a Bolshevist outbreak in the city of Seattle, over which he rules as mayor. A conglomeration of aliens from Russia and Finland attempted to give American "Bolshevism" an example by establishing a Soviet, in this Washington city, but Mayor Hanson, by the prompt announcement that the headquarters of the city government was the City Hall and that the first "reformer" to interfere with its operations would be shot, immediately dissolved the "revolution." The aliens who started the disturbance have been deported to their European homes.

Sunset, the Pacific Coast monthly, did not intend to lag behind its Eastern competitors: "Instead of crawling into the cyclone cellar, Seattle walked right up to the gate, a gun in either hand, to meet the Social Revolution. That in a nutshell is the reason why the Bolshevist upheaval did not take place according to schedule." . . .

Truth was, a revolutionary spark did exist in Seattle in February, 1919. The strike leaders knew that as well as the government, and were mortally frightened. For that reason unionists were ordered to remain at home and avoid any gatherings; the *Union Record* was ordered not to publish; no incident was to be permitted that might flare into provocation of the Army and the thousands of armed vigilantes. By the third day of the strike they realized that the Seattle labor movement stood all alone; the strike wave did not even spread down the coast to California nor was there any move across a nation falling under the spell of the anti-Red hysteria to give aid and comfort, even verbally, to the labor movements of Seattle and Tacoma. Seattle, unfortunately, was all too unique in its militancy.

QUESTIONS

1. What were the advantages of a general strike over a strike by just one union at just one workplace?
2. Why did the newspapers have such a hysterical reaction to the Seattle General strike? Whose interests did this serve?
3. Did the striking unions do the right thing by ending the strike so quickly? Why or why not?

35

A. J. Muste Mourns Slain
Textile Workers, 1929

The 1920s saw an exodus of jobs from textile mills in the North. Reacting to successful union organizing drives in northern mills, mill owners began moving their factories into southern states in the 1920s. Wages were lower in the rural South than the urban North, and local customs stressed shared interests between white workers and owners, as well as sharply drawn color lines that mitigated against interracial cooperation.

As early as the late 1920s, however, the oppressive conditions in southern mills had become intolerable, and mill workers began to form unions. In a knee-jerk reaction against labor unions, local law enforcement beat and killed local organizers in Gastonia and Marion, North Carolina. This document, a eulogy delivered by pacifist minister and American Federation of Teachers vice-president A. J. Muste, mourns the passing of six workers killed in Marion, and urges workers around the nation to support the families of the slain workers and learn from their example.

In the 1930s, the Congress of Industrial Organizations successfully organized workers in industries that had been resistant to unions. Despite their success in organizing automotive, steel, and rubber workers, CIO efforts in Southern textile mills in the 1940s were generally unsuccessful.

THESE MEN ARE good soldiers who have fallen in a war that is as old as humanity. They are martyrs in the noblest cause in all the

Excerpt from "Address of A. J. Muste," in *Progressive Labor Library Pamphlet No. 2*, "The Marion Murders" (New York: National Executive Committee of the Conference for Progressive Labor Action, 1929), 14–17.

world. The cause for which they died is the cause of labor, the cause of justice and freedom for the plain people who do the work of the world and who bear its burdens.

The struggle of the masses against those who exploit and oppress them is as old as history. Jesus found it going on in his day. He chose to side with the common people. Therefore, the good people of his day, the respectable people, the law-and-order gang, the church people, turned upon him. They said he was a revolutionist. They maligned his personal character and said he was a glutton and a drunkard and a friend of harlots. Because he was in their way they crucified him.

We must see to it that these martyrs of Marion shall not have died in vain. We shall not accomplish that by bitterness toward this individual or that, though if there were bitterness in any hearts today, I would not dare to sit in judgment upon them. Workers have slaved for a pittance in these mills. When they made a peaceful move to organize, their leaders were fired, thrown out on the street. When they had to choose between striking and losing their union, they struck. All the paraphernalia of the law, all the force of the state was used to crush their strike. When they made an agreement, it was violated, treated like a scrap of paper. When they refused to submit like whipped curs to such baseness and struck again, they were shot down in cold blood, one of them, a man who had endured 65 years of life under such conditions, known as one of the hardest and most faithful workers at the mill on a wage of $11.50 a week, was given the glorious reward of being brutally beaten and shot in the back by so-called officers of the law, and put on the operating table with handcuffs on him before he breathed his last. In the stormy history of labor in America there has been no blacker outrage than this. I say to all who are in any sense responsible for such outrages, officers of the law, owners of mills, the commonwealth of North Carolina— a system of industry and society which makes such things possible, what Jesus said to the mighty and prosperous of his day, "Woe unto you, if you offend one of these little ones. It were better for you that a millstone were tied around your neck and that you were cast into the midst of the sea."

The death of these comrades is a challenge to the American Federation of Labor. Southern textile workers have in recent months been knocking at its doors clamoring to be organized. No such opportunity has confronted it in years. If the textile industry of the South is organized, other industries in the section will follow. With the growing industries of the South won for unionism, the labor movement could sweep the nation, could bring in a new day for the masses of workers in our basic industries, who suffer want in the midst of plenty.

But the A. F. of L. must have the will, the intelligence and the courage to seize the opportunity. It must meet the challenge that has been thrown down to it here. All the force of the state has been brought to bear against this effort to organize an A. F. of L. union in Marion. In Gastonia the excuse has been that the opposition was not against unionism but against communism. But no such outrage has been perpetrated against the communists in Gastonia as the unspeakable outrage which has been committed against an A. F. of L. union and its members in Marion.

The only adequate answer is an immediate, persistent, large-scale campaign to organize the textile workers of the South. Let the A. F. of L. in convention, the parliament of American labor, set the machinery in motion to raise immediately a fund of a million dollars in memory of the martyrs of Marion, for organization work and strike relief in the South. Then these dead shall not have died in vain.

QUESTIONS

1. How does Muste use Christian imagery to make his point?
2. What prevented more successful AFL organization in Southern textile mills?
3. How do you think the Marion murders affected the course of Southern union organizing?

36

Howard Kester on the Rout of the Southern Tenant Farmers' Union, 1935

The Southern Tenant Farmers' Union was a rare example of interracial union activity in the Southern states. Organizing workers in the cotton-growing belt of northern Arkansas from July 1934 to April 1935, the STFU fought for fair wages and business practices for sharecroppers. Sharecroppers often worked in a state of perpetual debt to landowners, without access to decent food, schooling, or medical care.

Radical journalist Howard Kester (1904–1977) traveled to Arkansas to call attention to the sharecroppers' plight. What follows is the story of the two-week "Arkansas Hurricane" of violence that basically ended the union's work.

MARCH 21ST.

A mob of approximately forty men, led by the manager of one of the largest plantations in Poinsett County, a town constable, a deputy sheriff, and composed of planters and riding bosses, attempted to lynch the Rev. A. B. Brookins, seventy-year-old Negro minister, chaplain of the union and a member of the National Executive Council.

After the mob had failed on four different occasions to lure Brookins from his cabin in Marked Tree, the mob turned their guns upon his home and riddled it with bullets. Brookins escaped in his night clothes while his daughter was shot through the head and his wife escaped death by lying prone upon the floor.

Excerpt from *Revolt Among the Sharecroppers* by Howard Kester. Copyright © 1997 by the University of Tennessee Press. Reprinted by permission.

March 21st.

W. H. Stultz, president of the Southern Tenant Farmers' Union, found a note on his doorsteps warning him to leave Poinsett County within twenty-four hours. This note, written on a typewriter, was signed with ten X's and said, "We have decided to give you twenty-four hours to get out of Poinsett County."

On the following day Stultz was taken into the offices of the Chapman-Dewey Land Company by A. C. Spellings, Fred Bradsher and Bob Frazier on a pretext that Chief of Police Shannabery wanted to see him. While in the offices guns were laid upon a nearby barrel by the vigilantes and efforts were made by them to get Stultz to give them a pretext whereby to kill him. After being detained for three hours he was told by one of the men that he would "personally see to it that if you don't leave town that your brains are blown out and your body thrown in the St. Francis River." Stultz, the father of six small children, had been a sharecropper until driven from the land because of union activities. Night riders terrorized his family and attempted to blow up his home and in order to save them from almost certain death he and his family were moved to Memphis by the union.

March 21st.

The Rev. T. A. Allen, Negro preacher and organizer of the union, was found shot through the heart and his body weighted with chains and rocks in the waters of the Coldwater River near Hernando, Mississippi. The sheriff informed the reporter of the United Press that Allen was probably killed by enraged planters and that there would be no investigation.

March 22nd.

Mrs. Mary Green, wife of a member of the union in Mississippi County, died of fright when armed vigilantes came to her home to lynch her husband who was active in organizing the sharecroppers in that county.

March 22nd.

After threatening Clay East, former president of the Southern Tenant Farmers' Union, and Miss Mary Hillyer, of New York, with violence if they addressed a meeting of the union in Marked Tree, a mob drove the two into the office of C. T. Carpenter, the union attorney, surrounded the building and blocked all exits. After requesting protection from the mayor, East agreed to talk with the mob. He was told that if he ever returned to Poinsett County that he would be shot on sight. Mayor Fox finally interceded with the mob which allowed Mr. East and Miss Hillyer to leave town but formed an armed band to escort them out of the county.

March 23rd.
An armed band of twenty or thirty men attempted to kill C. T. Carpenter of Marked Tree, attorney for the union, at his home shortly before midnight. The leaders of the mob demanded that Carpenter give himself up but this he refused to do. With gun in hand, Carpenter prevented the mob from breaking into his home. The presence of his wife probably prevented the mob from shooting directly at Carpenter, but as they departed they poured bullets into the porch and sides of the house, breaking out the lights.

On the following night a committee from the vigilantes called upon Mr. Carpenter in his office and threatened to shoot him there if he did not sever his connections with the union. This he refused to do.

An item in the *New York Times* reads: "A band of forty-odd night riders fired upon the home of C. T. Carpenter, southern Democrat, whose father fought with General Lee in the Army of the Confederacy. The raid was a climax to a similar attack upon the homes of Negro members of the union."

March 27th.
John Allen, secretary of the union on the Twist plantation in Cross County, escaped a mob of riding bosses and deputies, who were trying to lynch him, by hiding in the swamps around the St. Francis River.

During the frantic search for Allen numberous beatings occurred. When a Negro woman refused to reveal Allen's whereabouts her ear was severed from her head by a lick from the gun of a riding boss.

March 30th.
An armed band of vigilantes mobbed a group of Negro men and women who were returning home from church near Marked Tree. Both men and women were severely beaten by pistols and flashlights and scores of children were trampled underfoot by the members of the mob.

March 30th.
Walter Moskop, a member of the trio which toured the East in behalf of the union narrowly escaped a mob which had gathered about his home to lynch him. Moskop's eleven-year-old son overheard the conversation between the vigilantes and informed his father of the mob's intention just in time for him to be smuggled out of his home by friends.

April 2nd.
The home of the Rev. E. B. McKinney, vice-president of the union, was riddled with more than two hundred and fifty bullets from machine guns by vigilantes. McKinney's family and a number of friends were inside. Two occupants of the home were severely wounded and the family given until sunrise to get out of the county. The mob was looking for H. L. Mitchell and the author who were reported to be holding a meeting in McKinney's home at the time.

QUESTIONS

1. Could planters have treated sharecroppers this way if sharecroppers had been enslaved?
2. What factors might have determined whether a union member was lynched, driven out of town, or merely harassed?
3. How did the forces of law and order play a role in the "Arkansas Hurricane"?

37

Louis Adamic Lists the Virtues and Advantages of the Sitdown Strike, 1936

A sitdown strike differs from ordinary strikes in that workers do not leave the premises after it is called. Instead, they stay by their equipment to make sure that management cannot operate it in their place. If unable to restart operations, the theory goes, employers would be more likely to meet labor's demands. The Industrial Workers of the World pioneered the use of sitdown strikes, but the tactic became increasingly popular in the late 1930s, especially after the United Auto Workers used the tactic to gain recognition from General Motors in early 1937.

Here labor journalist Louis Adamic writes about the advantages of the sitdown strike in the abstract. Even as early as December 1936 (when he wrote this piece), he had many examples from which to draw his conclusions, especially in the rubber industry. Sitdown strikes became much less common after the United States Supreme Court declared them illegal in 1939. They still happen on occasion during American labor disputes, but workers who use the tactic are likely to face arrest.

1. THE SITDOWN IS the reverse of sabotage, to which many workers are opposed. It destroys nothing. Before shutting down a department in a rubber plant, for instance, the men take the compounded rubber from the mills, or they finish building or curing the tires then being built or cured, so that nothing is needlessly ruined. Taking the same precautions during the sitdown as they do during production, the men do not smoke

Excerpt from Louis Adamic, "Sitdown." Reprinted with permission from the December 6, 1936 issue of *The Nation*.

in departments where benzine is used. There is no drinking. This discipline—of which more in a moment—is instinctive.

2. To say, as did a New York *Times* reporter, writing from Akron in January 1936, that the sitdown "resembles the old Oriental practice of passive resistance" is a bit far-fetched, but it probably is a sort of development of the old I.W.W. "folded-arm" strike and of "striking on the job"; only it is better than the latter, which required men to pretend they were working, and to accomplish as little as possible without being discharged, which was more fatiguing than to work according to one's capacity, as well as contrary to the natural inclinations of the best class of the workers.

3. The sitdown is the reverse of the ordinary strike. When a sitdown is called, a man does not walk out; he stays in, implying that he is willing to work if——

4. Workers' wives generally object to regular strikes, which often are long, sometimes violent and dangerous, and as likely as not end in sellouts and defeat. Sitdowns are quick, short, and free of violence. There are no strike-breakers in the majority of instances; the factory management does not dare to get tough and try to drive the sitting men out and replace them with other workers, for such violence would turn the public against the employers and the police, and might result in damage to costly machinery. In a sitdown there are no picket-lines outside the factories, where police and company guards have great advantage when a fight starts. The sitdown action occurs wholly inside the plant, where the workers, who know every detail of the interior, have obvious advantages. The sitters-down organize their own "Police squads," arming them—in rubber—with crowbars normally used to pry open molds in which tires are cured. These worker cops patrol the belt, watch for possible scabs and stand guard near the doors: In a few instances where city police and company cops entered a factory, they were bewildered, frightened, and driven out by the "sitting" workers with no difficulty whatever.

5. Most workers distrust—if not consciously, then unconsciously—union officials and strike leaders and committees, even when they themselves have elected them. The beauty of the sitdown or the stay-in is that there are no leaders or officials to dis-

trust. There can be no sellout. Such standard procedure as strike sanction is hopelessly obsolete when workers drop their tools, their machines, and sit down beside them. The initiative, conduct, and control of the sitdown come directly from the men involved.

6. The fact that the sitdown gives the worker in mass-production industries a vital sense of importance cannot be overemphasized. Two sitdowns which completely tied up plants employing close to ten thousand men were started by half a dozen men each. Imagine the feeling of power those men experienced! And the thousands of workers who sat down in their support shared that feeling in varying degrees, depending on their individual power of imagination. One husky gum-miner said to me, "Now we don't feel like taking the sass off any snot-nose college-boy foreman." Another man said, "Now we know our labor is more important than the money of the stockholders, than the gambling in Wall Street, than the doings of the managers and foremen." One man's grievance, if the majority of his fellow-workers in his department agreed that it was a just grievance, could tie up the whole plant. He became a strike leader; the other members of the working force in his department became members of the strike committee. *They* assumed full responsibility in the matter: formed their own patrols, they kept the machines from being pointlessly destroyed, and they met with the management and dictated their terms. *They* turned their individual self-control and restraint into group self-discipline—which probably was the best aspect of the sitdown. *They* settled the dispute, not some outsider.

7. Work in most of the departments of a rubber factory or any other kind of mass-production factory is drudgery of the worst sort—mechanical and uncreative, insistent and requiring no imagination; and any interruption is welcomed by workers, even if only subconsciously. The conscious part of their mind may worry about the loss of pay; their subconscious, however, does not care a whit about that. The sitdown is dramatic, thrilling.

8. All these factors were important in the early sitdowns. They are still important. In addition, now there is in Akron the three-year-old tradition that when a sitdown begins anywhere along

the line of production everybody else was to sit down, too. And while we are explaining the men's solidarity in sitdowns, I must not forget also that the average worker in a mass-production plant is full of grievances and complaints, some of them hardly realized, and he knows or feels instinctively that when he and his fellow workers get ready to act, they will need the support of all the labor in the place and they will get it only if they back the men who have initiated the sitdown.

9. The sitdown is a purely democratic action, as democracy is understood in America within the capitalist system.

10. The sitdown is a social affair. Sitting workers talk. They get acquainted. And they like that. In a regular strike it is impossible to bring together under one roof more than one or two thousand people, and these only for a meeting, where they do not talk with one another but listen to speakers. A rubber sitdown holds under the same roof up to ten or twelve thousand idle men, free to talk among themselves, man to man. "Why, my God, man," one Goodyear gum-miner told me in November 1936, "during the sitdowns last spring I found out that the guy who works next to me is the same as I am, even if I was born in West Virginia and he is from Poland. His grievances are the same. Why shouldn't we stick?"

QUESTIONS

1. What were the advantages of sitdown strikes over regular strikes?
2. What aspects of the sitdown strikes brought workers from diverse backgrounds together?
3. Why do you think the Supreme Court ruled sitdown strikes illegal?

Working-Class Culture

McSorley's Bar, 1912, John Sloan.
Founders Society Purchase, General Membership Fund.
Photograph © 1987, The Detroit Institute of Arts.

Lester Hunter, "I'd Rather Not Be on Relief," 1938

During the mid-1930s, thousands of farmers and farmworkers fled their homes on the Great Plains of the South Central United States to escape the devastating effects of the Dust Bowl, the worst drought in this nation's history. Most headed to California in the hopes of finding jobs as harvest workers there. Unfortunately, there were far too many people chasing after too few jobs. Franklin D. Roosevelt created the Farm Security Agency in 1937 to help these and other migrant workers. One of the FSA's functions was to create camps to house the workers.

Charles L. Todd and Robert Sonkin spent the summer of 1940 and 1941 taping songs, conversations, meetings and stories of migrant workers in Central California for the Library of Congress. Only the transcript of a song they recorded at the Shafter refugee camp still exists. Nothing is known of the author, but many victims of the Depression shared his desire for economic opportunities.

> We go around all dressed in rags
> While the rest of the world goes neat,
> And we have to be satisfied
> With half enough to eat.
> We have to live in lean-tos,
> Or else we live in a tent,

Excerpt from Lester Hunter, "I'd Rather Not Be on Relief," 1938. American Memory, Library of Congress, Washington, D.C. *Voices from the Dust Bowl: The Charles L. Todd and Robert Sonkin Migrant Worker Collection, 1940–1941.*

For when we buy our bread and beans
There's nothing left for rent.

I'd rather not be on the rolls of relief,
Or work on the W. P. A.,
We'd rather work for the farmer
If the farmer could raise the pay;
Then the farmer could plant more cotton
And he'd get more money for spuds,
Instead of wearing patches,
We'd dress up in new duds.

From the east and west and north and south
Like a swarm of bees we come;
The migratory workers
Are worse off than a bum.
We go to Mr. Farmer
And ask him what he'll pay;
He says, "You gypsy workers
Can live on a buck a day."

I'd rather not be on the rolls of relief,
Or work on the W. P. A.,
We'd rather work for the farmer
If the farmer could raise the pay;
Then the farmer could plant more cotton
And he'd get more money for spuds,
Instead of wearing patches,
We'd dress up in new duds.

We don't ask for luxuries
Or even a feather bed.
But we're bound to raise the dickens
While our families are underfed.
Now the winter is on us
And the cotton picking is done,
What are we going to live on
While [we're waiting] for spuds to come?

Now if you will excuse me
I'll bring my song to an end.
I've got to go and chuck a crack
Where the howling wind comes in.
The times are going to better
And I guess you'd like to know
I'll tell you all about it,
I've joined the C. I. O.

QUESTIONS

1. Does Hunter blame someone else or himself for his predicament? Explain.
2. What does this song tell you about attitudes toward government welfare in the farm camps of the 1930s?
3. Was joining the CIO a good solution for the migrant worker's problems in the 1930s? Was unionizing migrant farm workers even feasible?

Vivian Morris Interviews
an Unemployed Domestic
at the "Bronx Slave Market," 1938

During the Depression, the Roosevelt Administration paid unemployed writers to capture the personal histories of ordinary people all across America. A group of unemployed African American authors conducted a series of interviews in New York City's Harlem neighborhood, which was probably the most important concentration of black culture in the entire country. A decade earlier, Harlem had been a bustling middle-class community, particularly noteworthy for the many artists, musicians, and writers who lived there. That changed during the Great Depression, which hit African Americans, even the most affluent among them, particularly hard.

Vivian Morris worked for the Federal Writers Project, an arm of the larger Works Progress Administration, the New Deal agency that hired many struggling Americans. Here she describes a group of people whose needs were not addressed by government programs. Domestic service has never been lucrative. The Great Migration, which brought African Americans from the South to places like Harlem in the 1910s and 1920s, exacerbated the tough competition that domestics in the North already faced. There were many people desperate enough to work hard on a temporary basis for very low wages, and not enough of these jobs to go around.

HAVING HEARD rumors that a "Slave Market" was in existence in the Bronx—according to hearsay, this market was operated by white "Madams" where Negro women slaved for a few cents per day—

Excerpt from Vivian Morris, "Bronx Slave Market," American Memory, Library of Congress, Washington, D.C. *American Life Histories: Manuscripts from the Federal Writers' Project, 1936–1940.*

early one November morning, I decided to confirm such reports by making a personal tour of the neighborhood where the condition was supposed to exist.

While walking down 167th St. and as I reached Girard Ave., I found the object of my search. Here I was confronted by sites and tales of woe which I shall always remember.

There, seated on crates and boxes, were a dejected gathering of Negro women of various ages and descriptions—youths of seventeen, and elderly women of maybe seventy. These women were scantily attired—some still wearing summer clothing—and as the November wind swept and whistled through them, they ducked their heads and tried to huddle within themselves as they pushed close to the wall.

I joined the group as though in quest of a job. Although properly clothed, I too, suffered from the bitter cold which made me shift from foot to foot. Immediately, my thoughts strayed to these twenty or more unfortunate women who were partly-clothed, some with tennis shoes, cut-out men's shoes, warped women's shoes bearing Wanamaker's seals—the cast-offs of some forgotten "Madam."

A woman with a gold tooth smiled and invited me to share her box. Her face bore cuts over both eyes and the corner of her mouth. She appeared to be as broad as she was tall, but, despite all of this, her flat face bore a kindly expression. When she discovered that I was in her category, she became sympathetic and as one woman to another, she began to relate her futile struggle of life from past to present in my receptive ears. She commenced by stating that her name was "Minnie." Minnie was born in the tidewater section of Virginia near Norfolk, a seaport town, in 1908. (She looked forty-five). Her father was a black sailor "brawny of arm and smooth of tongue"—so her mother told her. . . . She decided to take a fling at marriage at the age of sixteen. She married a hard-drinking sailor thrice her age who gave her, for a wedding present, Fifty Dollars, and told her, "Get some puddy clo's fo' you' se'f." Minnie, unaccustomed to such a large amount of money, decided to save it—first having the satisfaction to touch, feel and count. The next night, her husband returned home roaring drunk and demanding money—"Five Dollars"—and when Minnie timidly took the roll from under her pillow and peeled off the requested amount, he attac[k]ed her insanely, cutting both her eyes and mouth knocking out her front teeth and taking all of the money. . . . She never saw him again!

During the next twelve years, Minnie worked steadier, became adjusted to conditions and was now a squat muscular woman whose endurance was beyond the average, and she could now work unlimited hours without audible protest. . . .

In September, 1938, Minnie having saved Twenty Dollars, decided to migrate to New York. She arrived with about six Dollars and paid four for a room, leaving two, and though, very hungry, was afraid to spend money for food that night. Early next morning, Minnie went to an Employment Agency. "Yes, they had jobs at Forty Dollars, sleep in or out." She almost shouted for joy—that was more money than she could make in Norfolk in two months! But this was New York. The Employment Agent signed Minnie up as a good cook-houseworker, etc., then he profferred her a card, saying: "Four Dollars, please."

Minnie said, her 'shoulders sagged!'

"Fo' Dollas fo' whut?"

"For the job; ya don't think I run this agency for my health, do you?" . . .

Minnie tried agency after agency but the results were the same. They wanted their money in front. She couldn't get day's or part-time work because the agents had special cliques to whom these choice jobs went. It was rank folly for any outsider to think of getting one of these jobs. After many days of trying, rent due, money gone, a sympathetic girl in one of the Agencies, told Minnie that, "when she was out of money, she stood on one of the corners in the Bronx, where women came and hired you." . . .

A weazened little woman, with aquiline nose, thick glasses and three big diamonds which seemed to laugh at the prominent-veined hands which were on passed down the line, critically looking at the girls. When she reached Minnie, she stopped peering: "Can you woik-hart voik? Can you vash windows from de houtside?"

"Ah c'n do anything—wash windows, anywhere." Time was passing, she had to get a job or be put out.

"Twenty-fife sants an hour?"

"No ma'am; thirty-five."

"I can get the youngk goils for fifteen sants, and the old vimmen for tan sants." She motioned towards the others who were eagerly crowding around. . . .

"But dey caint do de wokk Ah kin do," rebutted Minnie defiantly.

"Thirty-sants", said the bargain-hunter with an air of finality.

"Le's go," said Minnie flashing me a gold-toothed smile.

"See y'u latuh, honey. Ta'k to some o' de othah gals 'bout dere troublees. Sho' he'p yo' wile yo' time 'way."

So long, "Minnie,"

"Hope yo' don' meet no heifer lak' ah did on mah fus' job," she added.

I waved goodbye to the "slave" for a day. . . .

QUESTIONS

1. What accounts for the desperate position that women like Minnie faced? Was it just their race or were there other factors?
2. Why did these women all sit on the same corner? Would they have done better looking for work on their own? Why or why not?
3. Is it fair to compare Minnie's situation to that of antebellum slaves? Why or why not?

40

Leadbelly, Songs of Depression and War, 1938 and 1944

Huddie Ledbetter (1885–1949) grew up in Louisiana and worked in the turpentine camps of the western part of that state. The turpentine camps of eastern Texas and western Louisiana were fertile ground for the development of the blues, music derived from African American folksongs spawned in the era of slavery. Although blues songs begin with some kind of sad or unfortunate event, they generally end with humorous, life-affirming, or powerful statements that counteract the sadness. By the 1920s, Ledbetter became an acclaimed blues performer among his fellow workers.

However, he ran afoul of Jim Crow justice. In the 1930s, Ledbetter found himself in Louisiana's notorious Parchman Farm prison, a victim of trumped-up murder charges. Folklorist John Lomax, touring the rural South collecting songs for the Library of Congress, discovered Ledbetter's talent while recording Parchman singers. After he composed a song praising Louisiana governor O. K. Allen, Ledbetter won his release from prison, and promptly became a folk-music star. Ledbetter became a popular entertainer at labor rallies and anti-fascist benefits.

In the first of the two songs below, Ledbetter sings about his experiences in Washington, DC, where he and some white friends were unable to cross the color line to socialize in public. The second song expresses male resentment over women's newfound employment opportunities in wartime.

Excerpt from Leadbelly (Huddie Ledbetter), *Lead Belly: No Stranger to the Blues* (New York: Folkways Music Publishing, Inc., 1998), 6, 22.

"BOURGEOIS BLUES," 1938

Chorus:
Oh, he's a bourgeois man
Living in a bourgeois town.
I got the bourgeois blues,
And I'm sure gonna spread the news.

Me and Miss Barnicle went all over town:
I heard a colored man say, "You can't come around."
(Chorus)

Me and Martha were standin' upstairs;
I heard a white man say, "I don't want no niggers up
    there."
(Chorus)

I'm gonna tell all the colored people, I want 'em to
    understand;
Washington ain't no place for the colored man.
'Cause it's a bourgeois town.
(Chorus)

The white folks in Washington, they know how
To chuck you a nickel, just to see a nigger bow.
'Cause it's a bourgeois town,
(Chorus)

(alternate verses)
Me and my wife run all over town,
Everywhere we go the people would turn us down.

Home of the brave, land of the free,
I don't wanna be mistreated by no bourgoisie.

(alternate chorus)
Lord, it's a bourgeois town.
Whee, it's a bourgeois town.
I got the bourgeois blues.
I'm gonna spread the news all around.

"National Defense Blues," 1944

I had a little woman working on the national defense (2x)
That woman got to the place, act like she did not have no
    sense.

Just because she was working, making so much dough
That woman got to the place where she did not love me no
    more.

Every payday come, her check was big as mine
That woman thought that defense work's gonna last all the
    time.

Now the defense is gone, listen to my song
Since that defense been gone that woman done lose her
    home.

I will tell you the truth and it's got to be the fact
Since that defense been gone that woman lose her
    Cadillac.

I'm gonna tell you people, tell you as a friend
I don't believe that defense will ever be back again.

Questions

1. In what ways does Ledbetter's race shape the experiences he
   relates in "Bourgeois Blues"? In what way does his class shape
   those same experiences?
2. How would the woman discussed in "National Defense Blues"
   sing her version of the blues? In other words, how would she
   reply to Ledbetter's narrator?
3. To what extent do the themes of Ledbetter's songs still reso-
   nate in popular music?

Joseph Mitchell on McSorley's Saloon, 1940

Joseph Mitchell wrote for The New Yorker *magazine from 1933 to 1964. Although the magazine made its reputation for its coverage of high society, Mitchell made his reputation covering interesting personalities from New York's poor and working classes. Here Mitchell writes about a place rather than an individual: McSorley's saloon. In 1940, it remained much the same as it had been around the turn of the century and still remains much the same way today.*

In the nineteenth century, saloons were the center of immigrant life in cities like New York. Saloonkeepers were often political leaders, and many of the decisions that determined the fate of communities were made in establishments like McSorley's. If home was a crowded and dirty tenement, workers might opt to spend more time in the saloon than they did with their families. Although paintings and sketches of McSorley's, like the one on page 165, have made it just about the most famous saloon in the nation, it still serves as an example of the kind of working-class gathering place that dotted cities and towns across the United States during the late nineteenth and early twentieth centuries.

MCSORLEY'S OCCUPIES the ground floor of a red-brick tenement at 15 Seventh Street, just off Cooper Square, where the Bowery ends. It was opened in 1854 and is the oldest saloon in New York City. In eighty-eight years it has had four owners—an Irish immigrant, his son, a retired policeman, and his daughter—and all of them have been opposed to change. It is equipped with electricity, but

From *Up in the Old Hotel* by Joseph Mitchell, © 1992 by Joseph Mitchell. Used by permission of Pantheon Books, a division of Random House, Inc.

the bar is stubbornly illuminated with a pair of gas lamps, which flicker fitfully and throw shadows on the low, cobwebby ceiling each time someone opens the street door. There is no cash register. Coins are dropped in soup bowls—one for nickels, one for dimes, one for quarters, and one for halves—and bills are kept in a rosewood cashbox. It is a drowsy place; the bartenders never make a needless move, the customers nurse their mugs of ale, and the three clocks on the walls have not been in agreement for many years. The clientele is motley. It includes mechanics from the many garages in the neighborhood, salesmen from the restaurant-supply houses on Cooper Square, truck-drivers from Wanamaker's, internes from Bellevue, students from Cooper Union, and clerks from the row of second-hand bookshops just north of Astor Place. The backbone of the clientele, however, is a rapidly thinning group of crusty old men, predominantly Irish, who have been drinking there since they were youths and now have a proprietary feeling about the place. Some of them have tiny pensions, and are alone in the world; they sleep in Bowery hotels and spend practically all their waking hours in McSorley's. A few of these veterans clearly remember John McSorley, the founder, who died in 1910 at the age of eighty-seven. They refer to him as Old John, and they like to sit in rickety armchairs around the big belly stove which heats the place, gnaw on the stems of their pipes, and talk about him.

Old John was quirky. He was normally affable but was subject to spells of unaccountable surliness during which he would refuse to answer when spoken to. He went bald in early manhood and began wearing scraggly, patriarchal sideburns before he was forty. Many photographs of him are in existence, and it is obvious that he had a lot of unassumed dignity. He patterned his saloon after a public house he had known in his hometown in Ireland—Omagh, in County Tyrone—and originally called it the Old House at Home; around 1908 the signboard blew down, and when he ordered a new one he changed the name to McSorley's Old Ale House. That is still the official name; customers never have called it anything but McSorley's. Old John believed it impossible for men to drink with tranquillity in the presence of women; there is a fine back room in the saloon, but for many years a sign was nailed on the street door, saying, "NOTICE. NO

BACK ROOM IN HERE FOR LADIES." In McSorley's entire history, in fact, the only woman customer ever willingly admitted
was an addled old peddler called Mother Fresh-Roasted, who
claimed her husband died from the bite of a lizard in Cuba during
the Spanish-American War and who went from saloon to saloon
on the lower East Side for a couple of generations hawking pea-
nuts, which she carried in her apron. On warm days, Old John
would sell her an ale, and her esteem for him was such that she
embroidered him a little American flag and gave it to him one
Fourth of July; he had it framed and placed it on the wall above
his brass-bound ale pump, and it is still there. When other women
came in, Old John would hurry forward, make a bow, and say,
"Madam, I'm sorry, but we don't serve ladies." If a woman insisted, Old John would take her by the elbow, head her toward
the door, and say, "Madam, please don't provoke me. Make haste
and get yourself off the premises, or I'll be bliged to forget you're
a lady." This technique, pretty much word for word, is still in use.

In his time, Old John catered to the Irish and German workingmen—carpenters, tanners, bricklayers, slaughter-house butch-
ers, teamsters, and brewers—who populated the Seventh Street
neighborhood, selling ale in pewter mugs at five cents a mug and
putting out a free lunch inflexibly consisting of soda crackers,
raw onions, and cheese; present-day customers are wont to complain that some of the cheese Old John laid out on opening night
in 1854 is still there. Adjacent to the free lunch he kept a quart
crock of tobacco and a rack of clay and corncob pipes—the purchase of an ale entitled a man to a smoke on the house; the rack
still holds a few of the communal pipes. Old John was thrifty and
was able to buy the tenement—it is five stories high and holds
eight families—about ten years after he opened the saloon in it.
He distrusted banks and always kept his money in a cast-iron
safe; it still stands in the back room, but its doors are loose on
their hinges and there is nothing in it but an accumulation of
expired saloon licenses and several McSorley heirlooms, including Old John's straight razor. . . .

Although Old John did not consider himself retired until just
a few years before he died, he gave up day-in-and-day-out duty
back of the bar around 1890 and made his son, [Bill McSorley],
head bartender. . . .

At midday McSorley's is crowded. The afternoon is quiet. At six it fills up with men who work in the neighborhood. Most nights there are a few curiosity-seekers in the place. If they behave themselves and don't ask too many questions, they are tolerated. The majority of them have learned about the saloon through John Sloan's paintings. Between 1912 and 1930, Sloan did five paintings, filled with detail, of the saloon—"McSorley's Bar," which shows Bill presiding majestically over the tap and which hangs in the Detroit Institute of Arts; "McSorley's Back Room," a painting of an old workingman sitting at the window at dusk with his hands in his lap, his pewter mug on the table; "McSorley's at Home," which shows a group of argumentative old-timers around the stove; "McSorley's Cats," in which Bill is preparing to feed his drove of cats; and "McSorley's, Saturday Night," which was painted during prohibition and shows Bill passing out mugs to a crowd of rollicking customers. Every time one of these appears in an exhibition or in a newspaper or magazine, there is a rush of strangers to the saloon. "McSorley's Bar" was reproduced in Thomas Craven's "A Treasury of Art Masterpieces," which came out in 1939, and it caused hundreds to go and look the place over. There is no doubt that McSorley's has been painted more often than any other saloon in the country. Louis Bouché did a painting, "McSorley's," which is owned by the University of Nebraska. A painting, "Morning in McSorley's Bar," by a ship's purser named Ben Rosen won first prize in an exhibition of art by merchant seamen in February, 1943. Reginald Marsh has done several sketches of it. In 1939 there was a retrospective exhibition of Sloan's work in Wanamaker's art department, and a number of McSorley patrons attended it in a body. One asked a clerk for the price of "McSorley's Cats." "Three thousand dollars," he was told. He believed the clerk was kidding him and is still indignant.

QUESTIONS

1. What besides alcohol would have made McSorley's appealing to working-class patrons?
2. Why might it have been important for old John to keep women out of McSorley's?
3. Why do you think McSorley's appealed to artists so much?

Part IV: 1945–Present

IN THE YEARS FOLLOWING World War II, America went through an unprecedented economic boom that lasted into the early 1970s. Much of this prosperity rested on the spending of the federal government, which paid for returning veterans to go to school, provided high-paying defense jobs during the postwar military buildup, and built a new interstate highway system starting in 1956. But even before the boom ended, there were signs of difficult times ahead.

During the first years of the postwar prosperity, American workers could afford homes and more consumer goods like cars and refrigerators because they tended to have good jobs with good wages. Both these things were lacking during the Depression. The union movement was responsible for some of this prosperity because of its efforts on behalf of its member workers. However, union membership in the United States peaked at 25.4 percent of the workforce in 1954 and has been declining ever since. The 1955 reunification of the AFL and CIO was an indicator of the threat that organized labor saw to its position.

There are many contributing reasons for this decline. First, many workers in the postwar era entered the kinds of jobs in which unionization was strongly discouraged (see number 43, Whyte). Other, less-skilled workers held jobs in which they could easily be replaced (see number 42, Acuna). Naturally, if they could easily be replaced, workers seldom risked angering their employers by organizing or striking. American businesses also began to face increasing competition from firms overseas. Later on, this competition led to downsizing or the closing down of entire industries.

When the postwar prosperity ended in the early 1970s, America's manufacturing base began a long and steep decline. Economic stagflation made workers more timid, too. The increase in service jobs accompanying this change made American workers even less likely to organize. Fast-food employees, for example, tend not to care about their circumstances because they do not see this work as a career (see number 44, Leidner). Temporary workers, another recent economic phenomenon that more and more Americans have been forced to accept, have to put up with their circumstances to put food on the table (see number 53, "Keffo").

This does not mean that the kind of radicalism that once defined much of the American labor movement died in the late twentieth century. It either could not survive the conservative climate of the time or it took different forms. The United Electrical Workers, for example, suffered greatly for being a communist-controlled union during the McCarthy Era (see number 46, Lerner).

Privileged workers made some progress during this period. The growth of the personal computer and the Internet also did much to advance the lot of technologically adept workers as well as those who had the skills to program and fix this equipment. But these workers are still a minority of the American workforce. Furthermore, some of these innovations have led to technological unemployment (see number 45, Rifkin). As was the case in the era of industrialization, the proceeds of new technologies have flowed much more to employers than to their employees.

The area where workers have made the most progress in recent years is in recognizing and acting upon their common cultural ties. By preventing job discrimination on the basis of race or gender, the Civil Rights Act of 1964 provided the greatest legislative benefit to American workers between the passage of the Fair Labor Standards Act of 1937 and the present. As more women entered the workforce during the 1960s, many came to recognize the need to band together against gender discrimination (see number 50, "Judith Ann"). The Civil Rights Movement of the 1960s had great success in helping integrate African Americans into this country's political and social mainstream. However, by the late, 1960s black workers began to band together to make demands on the economic front (see number 49, Hamlin). Even the national AFL-CIO membership supported the sweeping reforms of the Civil Rights Act of 1964 (see number 48, Meany).

The cultural divisions of recent decades have also torn the working class apart in much the same way it has hurt the nation at large. The construction workers who attacked an antiwar protest in 1970 are symbolic of a more conservative strand of American life (see number 51, Cook). Antisocial behavior on the General Motors assembly line is indicative of the alienation that young workers sometimes experience on the job (see number 52, Hamper). When such cultural and generational differences cut through class lines, the chances for successful labor mobilization suffer greatly.

In recent years, there have been some signs that American labor is becoming more belligerent. For example, since becoming president of the AFL-CIO in 1995, John Sweeney has placed special emphasis on organizing unorganized workers. New blood in the leadership and the rank-and-file would create the potential for a new militancy. If this happens, the American working-class of the future would bear a greater resemblance to that of the past than the present.

Work and Labor/ Management Relations

Farm workers in one of the few remaining fields near the ocean in fast-growing Orange County, California, 1975.
Courtesy National Archives and Records Administration.

Roberto Acuna Recalls Life Growing Up as an Itinerant Farm Worker

*The situation that Mexican-American farm workers faced did not im-
prove between the Great Depression and the early 1960s because they,
unlike most factory workers, were not covered by New Deal labor
laws. Employers and their political supporters did not want the lowest wage workers in the American economy to have such protections.
The National Farm Workers Association (later the United Farm Workers of America), led by Cesar Chavez, would try to rectify these conditions starting in 1962. They signed the first collective bargaining
agreement in the history of American agriculture in 1966. Although
farm workers are now included under federal minimum wage provisions, they still have no rights to federal collective bargaining or over-
time pay.*

*Here, Roberto Acuna, an organizer for the United Farm Workers,
describes his early life in the fields of California, before the coming of
the union. Unlike the piece on Mexican fieldworkers that appears in
Part III of this collection, which was written by an outside observer,
here Acuna describes firsthand the exploitive conditions migrant workers endured. Even though he was only a child, Acuna had to work in
order to supplement the meager wages of his parents. Since the migrant
families were paid for piece work (by what they picked rather than by
the hour), even a child's physical labor could make a difference.*

I STARTED PICKING crops when I was eight. I couldn't do much but
every little bit counts. Every time I would get behind on my chores,
I would get a carrot thrown at me by my parents. I would day-

Excerpt from Studs Terkel, *Working* (New York: Pantheon Books, 1974), 33–36.
Reprinted by permission of Donadio & Olson, Inc. Copyright © 1974 by Studs
Terkel.

dream: If I were a millionaire, I would buy all these ranches and give them back to the people. I would picture my mom living in one area all the time and being admired by all the people living in the community. All of a sudden I would be rudely awakened by a broken carrot in my back. That would bust your whole dream apart and you'd work for a while and come back to daydreaming.

We used to work early, about four o'clock in the morning. We'd pick the harvest until about six. Then we'd run home and get into supposedly clean clothes and run all the way to school because we'd be late. By the time we got to school, we'd be all tuckered out. Around maybe eleven o'clock, we'd be dozing off. Our teachers would send notes to the house telling Mom that we were inattentive. The only thing I'd make fairly good grades on was spelling. I couldn't do anything else. Many times we never did our homework, because we were out in the fields. The teachers couldn't understand that. I would get whacked there also.

School would end maybe four o'clock. We'd rush home again, change clothes, go back to work until seven, seven thirty at night. That's not counting the weekends. On Saturday and Sunday, we'd be there from four thirty in the morning until about seven thirty in the evening. This is where we made the money, those two days. We all worked.

I would carry boxes for my mom to pack the carrots in. I would pull the carrots out and she would sort them into different sizes. I would get water for her to drink. When you're picking tomatoes, the boxes are heavy. They weigh about thirty pounds. They're dropped very hard on the trucks so they have to be sturdy.

The hardest work would be thinning and hoeing with a short-handled hoe. The fields would be about a half a mile long. You would be bending and stooping all day. Sometimes you would have hard ground and by the time you got home, your hands would be full of calluses. And you'd have a backache. Sometimes I wouldn't have dinner or anything. I'd just go home and fall asleep and wake up just in time to go out to the fields again.

I remember when we just got into California from Arizona to pick up the carrot harvest. It was very cold and very windy out in the fields. We just had a little old blanket for the four of us kids in the tent. We were freezin' our tails off. So I stole two brand-new blankets that belonged to a grower. When we got under those blankets it was nice and comfortable. Somebody saw me. The next morning the grower told my mom he'd turn us in unless we gave him back his blankets—sterilized. So my mom and I and my kid brother went to the river and cut some wood and made a fire and boiled the water and she scrubbed the blankets. She hung them out to dry, ironed them, and sent them back to the grower. We got a spanking for that.

I remember this labor camp that was run by the city. It was a POW camp for German soldiers. They put families in there and it would have barbed wire all around it. If you were out after ten o'clock at night, you couldn't get back until the next day at four in the morning. We didn't know the rules. Nobody told us. We went to visit some relatives. We got back at ten thirty and they wouldn't let us in. So we slept in the pickup outside the gate. In the morning, they let us in, we had a fast breakfast and went back to work in the fields.*

The grower would keep the families apart, hoping they'd fight against each other. He'd have three or four camps and he'd have the people over here pitted against the people over there. For jobs. He'd give the best crops to the people he thought were the fastest workers. This way he kept us working harder, competing.

When I was sixteen, I had my first taste as a foreman. Handling braceros, aliens, that came from Mexico to work. They'd bring these people to work over here and send them back to Mexico after the season was over. My job was to make sure they did a good job and pushin' 'em ever harder. I was a company man, yes. My parents needed money and I wanted to make sure they was proud of me. A foreman is recognized. I was very naïve. Even though I was pushing the workers, I knew their problems. They didn't know how to write, so I would write letters home for them. I would take 'em to town, buy their clothes outside of the company stores. They had paid me $1.10 an hour. The farm workers wage was raised to eighty-two and a half cents. But even the braceros were making more money than me, because they were working piecework. I asked for more money. The manager said, "If you don't like it you can quit." I quit and joined the Marine Corps. . . .

*Since we started organizing, this camp has been destroyed. They started building housing on it.

I began to see how everything was so wrong. When growers can have an intricate watering system to irrigate their crops but they don't have running water inside the houses of workers. Veterinarians tend to the needs of domestic animals but they can't have medical care for the workers. They can have land subsidies for the growers but they can't have adequate employment compensation for the workers. They treat him like a farm implement. In fact, they treat their implements better and their domestic animals better. They have insulated barns for the animals but the workers live in beat-up shacks with no heat at all.

QUESTIONS

1. If children have the opportunity to go to school, but their parents need the money, is it right for parents to let their children work in the fields?
2. Why might farm workers have put up with these kinds of conditions? Didn't they have better employment choices?
3. Would white workers have been treated this way?

William Whyte Defines
"The Organization Man," 1957

*Prosperity lifted most Americans to new heights of success in the post–
World War II United States. Manufacturing (or blue-collar) workers
used trade unions as vehicles to improve their economic status. Office
workers and middle managers (known as white-collar workers) improved their circumstances by attaching themselves to companies at
the forefront of the era's unprecedented economic boom. Although these
people are not generally thought of as working class, as their ranks
expanded after 1945 their situation came to resemble that of their
blue-collar brethren.*

   In his 1957 bestseller, The Organization Man, *the sociologist
William Whyte considers the plight of white-collar corporate employees in the postwar era. Here, at the very beginning of the book, he
tries to define his title and explain how large corporate bureaucracies
in the 1950s began to blur class lines.*

THIS BOOK IS ABOUT THE ORGANIZATION MAN. IF THE TERM IS VAGUE, it is
because I can think of no other way to describe the people I am
talking about. They are not the workers, nor are they the white-
collar people in the usual, clerk sense of the word. These people
only work for The Organization. The ones I am talking about
belong to it as well. They are the ones of our middle class who
have left home, spiritually as well as physically, to take the vows
of organization life, and it is they who are the mind and soul of
our great self-perpetuating institutions. Only a few are top managers or ever will be. In a system that makes such hazy terminol-

Excerpt from William H. Whyte, *The Organization Man.* Copyright © 1956 William
H. White, Jr. Reprinted by permission of the University of Pennsylvania Press.

ogy as "junior executive" psychologically necessary, they are of the staff as much as the line, and most are destined to live poised in a middle area that still awaits a satisfactory euphemism. But they are the dominant members of our society nonetheless. They have not joined together into a recognizable elite—our country does not stand still long enough for that—but it is from their ranks that are coming most of the first and second echelons of our leadership, and it is their values which will set the American temper.

The corporation man is the most conspicuous example, but he is only one, for the collectivization so visible in the corporation has affected almost every field of work. Blood brother to the business trainee off to join Du Pont: is the seminary student who will end up in the church hierarchy, the doctor headed for the corporate clinic, the physics Ph.D. in a government laboratory; the intellectual on the foundation-sponsored team project, the engineering graduate in the huge drafting room at Lockheed, the young apprentice in a Wall Street law factory.

They are all, as they so often put it, in the same boat. Listen to them talk to each other over the front lawns of their suburbia and you cannot help but be struck by how well they grasp the common denominators which bind them. Whatever the differences in their organization ties, it is the common problems of collective work that dominate their attentions, and when the Du Pont man talks to the research chemist or the chemist to the army man, it is these problems that are uppermost. The word collective most of them can't bring themselves to use—except to describe foreign countries or organizations they don't work for—but they are keenly aware of how much more deeply beholden they are to organization than were their elders. They are wry about it, to be sure; they talk of the "treadmill," the "rat race," of the inability to control one's direction. But they have no great sense of plight; between themselves and organization they believe they see an ultimate harmony and, more than most elders recognize, they are building an ideology that will vouchsafe this trust. . . .

Officially, we are a people who hold to the Protestant Ethic. Because of the denominational implications of the term many would deny its relevance to them, but let them eulogize the American Dream, however, and they virtually define the Protestant Ethic. Whatever the embroidery, there is almost always the thought that pursuit of individual salvation through hard work, thrift, and competitive struggle is the heart of the American achievement.

But the harsh facts of organization life simply do not jibe with these precepts. This conflict is certainly not a peculiarly American development. In their own countries such Europeans as Max Weber and Durkheim many years ago foretold the change, and though Europeans now like to see their troubles as an American export, the problems they speak of stem from a bureaucratization of society that has affected every Western country.

It is in America, however, that the contrast between the old ethic and current reality has been most apparent and most poignant. Of all peoples it is we who have led in the public worship of individualism. One hundred years ago De Tocqueville was noting that though our special genius—and failing—lay in co-operative action, we talked more than others of personal independence and freedom. We kept on, and as late as the twenties, when big organization was long since a fact, affirmed the old faith as if nothing had really changed at all.

Today many still try, and it is the members of the kind of organization most responsible for the change, the corporation, who try the hardest. It is the corporation man whose institutional ads protest so much that Americans speak up in town meeting, that Americans are the best inventors because Americans don't care that other people scoff, that Americans are the best soldiers because they have so much initiative and native ingenuity, that the boy selling papers on the street corner is the prototype of our business society. Collectivism? He abhors it, and when he makes his ritualistic attack on Welfare Statism, it is in terms of a Protestant Ethic undefiled by change—the sacredness of property, the enervating effect of security, the virtues of thrift, of hard work and independence. Thanks be, he says, that there are some people left—e.g., businessmen—to defend the American Dream.

He is not being hypocritical, only compulsive. He honestly wants to believe he follows the tenets he extols, and if he extols them so frequently it is, perhaps, to shut out a nagging suspicion that he, too, the last defender of the faith, is no longer pure. Only by using the language of individualism to describe the collective can he stave off the thought that he himself is in a collective as pervading as any ever dreamed of by the reformers, the intellectuals, and the utopian visionaries he so regularly warns against.

Questions

1. In what ways do the circumstances of Organization Men resemble those of other workers we have examined in this book? In what ways do they differ?
2. Do you agree with Whyte that working for a large organization is somehow "Un-American?" Why or why not?
3. Is the potential promise of the "American Dream" worth sacrificing your individuality to a large organization? Why or why not?

44

Robin Leidner Works at McDonald's, 1980s

Beginning in the late 1970s, the American economy began a profound shift away from manufacturing and toward service occupations. Service occupations often involve dealing with customers, which can require a great deal more creativity on the part of workers than monitoring an assembly line. However, large service-industry companies, particularly fast-food restaurants, pioneered methods of streamlining service work, to maximize efficiency and increase profits.

McDonald's is not only an icon of American culture, it is one of the largest employers in the United States. In the mid-1980s, sociologist Robin Leidner studied the impact of standardization on McDonald's workers in the Chicago area. Her fieldwork included working at a Chicago-area restaurant and sitting in on meetings with local franchise owners and managers. In this excerpt, she describes how McDonald's managers motivated their workers to do difficult, repetitive tasks.

CONDSIDERING WORKERS' LOW WAGES and limited stake in the success of the enterprise, why did they work so hard? Their intensity of effort was produced by several kinds of pressures. First, it seemed to me that most workers did conceive of the work as a team effort and were loath to be seen by their peers as making extra work for other people by not doing their share. Even workers who had what managers would define as a "bad attitude"—resentment

Excerpt from Robin Leidner, *Fast Food, Fast Talk: Service Work and the Routinization of Everyday Life* (Berkeley: University of California Press, © 1993 The Regents of the University of California), 77–80.

about low wages, disrespectful treatment, or any other issue—
might work hard in order to keep the respect of their peers.

Naturally, managers played a major role in keeping crew
people hard at work. At this store, managers were virtually always present behind the counter and in the grill area. During
busy periods several managers would be there at once, working
side by side with the crew as well as issuing instructions. Any
slacking off by a worker was thus very likely to be noticed. Managers insisted on constant effort; they clearly did not want to pay
workers for a moment of nonproductive time. For instance, I heard
a manager reprimand a grill worker for looking at the work schedule: "Are you off work? No? You look at the schedule on your
time, not on my time." A handwritten sign was posted recom-
mending that window workers come in fifteen minutes early to
count out the money in their cash-register drawers on their own
time so that, if the amount was wrong, they would not later be
held responsible for a shortage. Crew trainers and crew chiefs
were encouraged to let managers know about any workers who
were shirking or causing problems.

The presence of customers on the scene was another major
factor in intensifying workers' efforts. When long lines of people
were waiting to be served, few workers had to be told to work as
swiftly as possible. The sea of expectant faces provided a great
deal of pressure to keep moving. Window workers in particular
were anxious to avoid antagonizing customers, who were likely
to take out any dissatisfactions on them. The surest way to keep
people happy was to keep the lines moving quickly. The arrangement of the workplace, which made window workers clearly
visible to the waiting customers as they went about their duties,
and customers clearly visible to workers, was important in keeping crew people hard at work. This pressure could have an effect
even if customers did not complain. For example, on the day I
was to be trained to work window during breakfast, I spent quite
a while standing behind the counter, in uniform, waiting to be
put to work. I was acutely aware that customers were likely to
wonder why I did not take their orders, and I tried to adopt an air
of attentive expectancy rather than one of casual loitering, in the
hope that the customers would assume there was a good reason
for my idleness.

These sorts of pressures were not the only reasons crew people worked hard and enthusiastically, however. Managers also tried to motivate them to strenuous efforts through positive means. The managers' constant presence meant that good work would not go unnoticed. McDonald's Corporation stresses the importance of acknowledging workers' efforts, and several workers mentioned that they appreciated such recognition. Indeed, I was surprised at how much it cheered me when a manager complimented me on my "good eye contact" with customers. Various incentive systems were in place as well, to make workers feel that it was in their individual interest to work hard. Free McDonald's meals (instead of the usual half-priced ones) and free record albums were some of the rewards available to good workers. Contests for the highest sales totals or most special raspberry milk shakes sold in a given hour encouraged window workers to compete in speed and pushiness. The possibility of promotion to crew trainer, crew chief, or swing manager also motivated some workers to work as hard as possible.

Group incentives seemed to be especially effective in motivating the crew. As part of a national advertising effort stressing service, all of the stores in McDonald's Chicago region competed to improve their speed. The owner of the store where I worked promised that if one of his stores came out near the top in this competition, the entire crew would be treated to a day at a large amusement park and the crew trainers would be invited for a day's outing on his yacht. The crew trainers and many other workers were very excited about this possibility and were willing to try to achieve unprecedented standards of speed. (They did not win the prize, but the crew of one of the owner's other stores did.) Some workers, though, especially the more disaffected ones, had no desire for either promotions or the low-cost rewards available and spoke derisively of them.

Managers also tried to make workers identify with the interests of the store, even when it clearly resulted in harder work for the same pay. At a monthly meeting for crew trainers, a manager acknowledged that workers were always asking why the store would not pay someone for an extra fifteen minutes to sweep up or do other such tasks not directly related to production, instead of making workers squeeze these tasks in around their main duties. He explained the importance to management of keeping labor costs down:

> "Say we use four extra hours a day—we keep extra people to [wash] the brown trays" or some other tasks. He reels off some calculations—"that's 120 hours a month, times—let's pay them the minimum wage—times twelve months. So that's 1,440 hours times $3.35, equals $4,825." There are oohs and aahs from the trainers—this sounds like a lot of money to them. I don't think it sounds like that much out of $1.5 million (which he had just said the store brought in annually). The manager went on, "So how do we get extra labor? By watching how we schedule. A $200 hour [an hour with $200 in sales], for instance, will go smoother with four window people, but three good people could do it. We save money, and then we can use it on other things, like training, for instance."

The crew trainers were willing to agree that it was only reasonable for the store to extract as much labor from them as possible, though resentments about overwork certainly did not disappear. The manager was also successful enough in getting the crew trainers to indentify with management that they were willing to give the names of crew people who were uncooperative.

Questions

1. How are the McDonald's managers' motivational strategies similar to Taylorism? How are they different?
2. Why do McDonald's workers seem to side with their managers?
3. To what extent have jobs you've held resembled Leidner's at McDonald's?

45 ————————————————————————————————

Jeremy Rifkin Explains the Reasons for Technological Unemployment in the Information Age, 1995

During the era of industrialization, manufacturers eliminated the need for skilled laborers by dividing their tasks into small functions and replacing them with machines. Recent advances in information technology achieve the same objective, only now, machines can take over the entire work task. Industrialization changed only the manufacturing sector of the economy, but new technological developments affected service workers and even middle managers.

Here, author Jeremy Rifkin describes the effects of computers on the American and world economy. To him, the effect of technology on corporate restructuring in coming years will have an even greater effect on most workers than the emergence of a global marketplace because these changes will not just make working conditions more difficult, they will cause widespread unemployment. That would likely lead to serious social unrest, perhaps even a return to the violent labor confrontations of the late-nineteenth and early-twentieth centuries. The footnotes for the works Rifkin cites in the text have been omitted.

RE-ENGINEERING

"RE-ENGINEERING" IS SWEEPING through the corporate community, making true believers out of even the most recalcitrant CEOs. Companies are quickly restructuring their organizations to make them computer friendly. In the process, they are eliminating lay-

Excerpt from "The End of Work," by Jeremy Rifkin, copyright © 1995 by Jeremy Rifkin. Used by permission of Jeremy P. Tarcher, an imprint of Penguin Group (USA), Inc.

ers of traditional management, compressing job categories, creating work teams, training employees in multilevel skills, shortening and simplifying production and distribution processes, and streamlining administration. The results have been impressive. In the United States, overall productivity jumped 2.8 percent in 1992, the largest rise in two decades. The giant strides in productivity have meant wholesale reductions in the workforce. Michael Hammer, a former MIT professor and prime mover in the restructuring of the workplace, says that re-engineering typically results in the loss of more than 40 percent of the jobs in a company and can lead to as much as a 75 percent reduction in a given company's workforce. Middle management is particularly vulnerable to job loss from re-engineering. Hammer estimates that up to 80 percent of those engaged in middle-management tasks are susceptible to elimination.

Across the entire U.S. economy, corporate re-engineering could eliminate between 1 million and 2.5 million jobs a year "for the foreseeable future," according to *The Wall Street Journal.* By the time the first stage of re-engineering runs its course, some studies predict a loss of up to 25 million jobs in a private sector labor force that currently totals around 90 million workers. In Europe and Asia, where corporate restructuring and technology displacement is beginning to have an equally profound impact, industry analysts expect comparable job losses in the years ahead. Business consultants like John C. Skerritt worry about the economic and social consequences of re-engineering. "We can see many, many ways that jobs can be destroyed," says Skerritt, "but we can't see where they will be created." Others, like John Sculley, formerly of Apple Computer, believe that the "reorganization of work" could be as massive and destabilizing as the advent of the Industrial Revolution. "This may be the biggest social issue of the next 20 years," says Sculley. Hans Olaf Henkel, the CEO of IBM Deutschland, warns, "There is a revolution underway."

Nowhere is the effect of the computer revolution and re-engineering of the workplace more pronounced than in the manufacturing sector. One hundred and forty-seven years after Karl Marx urged the workers of the world to unite, Jacques Attali, a French minister and technology consultant to socialist President François Mitterand, confidently proclaimed the end of the era of the working man and woman. "Machines are the new proletariat," proclaimed Attali. "The working class is being given its walking papers."

The quickening pace of automation is fast moving the global economy to the day of the workerless factory. Between 1981 and 1991, more than 1.8 million manufacturing jobs disappeared in the U.S. In Germany, manufacturers have been shedding workers even faster, eliminating more than 500,000 jobs in a single twelve-month period between early 1992 and 1993. The decline in manufacturing jobs is part of a long-term trend that has seen the increasing replacement of human beings in the work place. In the 1950s, 33 percent of all U.S. workers were employed in manufacturing. By the 1960s, the number of manufacturing jobs had dropped to 30 percent, and by the 1980s to 20 percent. Today, less than 17 percent of the workforce is engaged in blue collar work. Management consultant Peter Drucker estimates that employment in manufacturing is going to continue dropping to less than 12 percent of the U.S. workforce in the next decade. . . .

Although the number of blue collar workers continues to decline, manufacturing productivity is soaring. In the United States, annual productivity, which was growing at slightly over 1 percent per year in the early 1980s, has climbed to over 3 percent in the wake of the new advances in computer automation and the restructuring of the workplace. From 1979 to 1992, productivity increased by 35 percent in the manufacturing sector while the workforce shrank by 15 percent.

William Winpisinger, past president of the International Association of Machinists, a union whose membership has shrunk nearly in half as a result of advances in automation, cites a study by the International Metalworkers Federation in Geneva forecasting that within thirty years, as little as 2 percent of the world's current labor force "will be needed to produce all goods necessary for total demand." Yoneji Masuda, a principal architect of the Japanese plan to become the first fully computerized information based society, says that "in the near future, complete automation of entire plants will come into being, and during the next twenty to thirty years there will probably emerge . . . factories that require no manual labor at all."

While the industrial worker is being phased out of the economic process, many economists and elected officials continue to hold out hope that the service sector and white collar work will be able to absorb the millions of unemployed laborers in search of work. Their hopes are likely to be dashed. Automation and re-engineering are already replacing human labor across a wide swath of service related fields. The new "thinking machines" are capable of performing many of the mental tasks now performed by human beings, and at greater speeds. Andersen Consulting Company, one of the world's largest corporate restructuring firms, estimates that in just one service industry, commercial banking and thrift institutions, re-engineering will mean a loss of 30 to 40 percent of the jobs over the next seven years. That translates into nearly 700,00 jobs eliminated.

QUESTIONS

1. Do you agree that re-engineering "could be as massive and destabilizing as the advent of the Industrial Revolution"? Explain.
2. Is re-engineering good for America? Does anybody benefit from this trend besides corporate executives and stockholders?
3. Is there anything American workers can do to fight re-engineering? If so, what? If not, why not?

The Union
Movement

*Flight attendants picket in front of Northwest Airlines, 1970.
No. MJS-6171, courtesy the Wisconsin Historical Society, photo by
Milwaukee Journal Sentinel.*

James Lerner Remembers How McCarthyism Affected the United Electrical Workers

In the late 1940s and early 1950s, Cold War tensions led the federal government and state governments to devote inordinate amounts of attention to finding communists in a variety of American institutions. In 1947, the House of Representatives' Un-American Activities Committee (HUAC) held highly publicized hearings on Communist influence in Hollywood. In 1954, Senator Joe McCarthy chaired hearings that sought to find communists in the State Department and the U.S. Army. These efforts revealed little evidence of communist infiltration, but the labor movement was another story. Communists had played a major role in organizing during the 1930s, and even though the party was not as popular in the late 1940s as it had been, there were probably more communists in the labor movement than any other segment of American life. That said, there certainly were not enough to make the labor movement an arm of Soviet foreign policy, as many critics alleged at the time.

The United Electrical Workers Union (UE) was one of a limited number of successful unions that still had a substantial number of current and former communists among its members and leaders in the late 1940s. Even though these workers showed as much if not more loyalty to labor's cause than the union's noncommunist members, anticommunists in labor, management, and Congress made an issue of their presence in the UE and other unions. The requirement in the 1947 Taft-Hartley Act that trade union leaders sign affadavits that they were not communists is one example of this effort. Even though "dual unionism" is perhaps the cardinal sin of labor organiz-

Excerpt from James Lerner, "National UE: Corporate Target for Extinction,"
© 1981 *UE News.*

ing, the Congress of Industrial Organizations (CIO) created a new, anticommunist, less-militant union, the International Union of Electrical Workers (IUE), to drive the UE out of existence. Here, James Lerner, the managing editor of the UE's newspaper, recalls how employers such as General Electric took advantage of the political climate of the time to spur the eradication of the UE.

GENERAL ELECTRIC set 1949 as the year it would be rid of the UE. That was the year the CIO leadership chartered a group to split the UE. Senator Hubert Humphrey lent his liberal pretensions to the cause, even though he owed his earlier election as mayor of Minneapolis in large measure to UE's political activity. The UE was the largest union in that city. Seeing in Red-baiting the path to greater glory, Humphrey sponsored a bill to outlaw unions such as UE and the others that were resisting the attacks on the Bill of Rights.

The CIO splitters were accusing the companies and especially GE of not being vigorous enough in supporting the drive to destroy the UE. What was actually bothering them was their inability to win enough support from the rank-and-file, which knew how much it had gained from UE representation.

Testifying in favor of the proposed Humphrey law, the head of General Electric's law department, William J. Barron, and the head of its labor relations department, Lemuel Boulware, told the Humphrey-chaired Senate Labor subcommittee it was only the action taken by GE in filing petitions with the NLRB which made it possible for James B. Carey, president of the newly manufactured IUE, to get elections as quickly as he did and at many locations where, at the time, he probably had no membership. "In this situation and by simply taking no action at all, we had an obvious and easy way to embarrass Mr. Carey, delay the elections and put him to great financial expenses—if we had wanted to use it. We took Mr. Carey off the hook by promptly filing our own petitions for an NLRB election." In other words, General Electric told the NLRB that the UE no longer represented the company's employees.

The Labor Board picked up the cue and decided to set aside its basic rule that union representation could be challenged by elections only at the end of a contract. The Board, deciding to make the law fit the company's and the CIO's crime, decreed that where a "schism" existed in a plant, a union certification could be thrown out and new elections held during the life of an agreement. The new split-off getup did not have to show any support in a plant to get an election—GE did it for them.

The same rule was applied to the other former CIO unions if they were challenged by a rival group. (Just as readily as the NLRB adopted the "schism" rule, it dropped it sometime later, after the purpose had been achieved. It wasn't going to run the risk of having a genuine rank-and-file rebellion against corruption or betrayal using the rule for decent purposes.)

At the Stewart-Warner plant in Chicago, where UE had won collective bargaining rights in 1943, the company coordinated its anti-union activities with a raid by a corrupt local of the IBEW six years later. The UE was denied a place on the ballot because its officers had refused to sign the Taft-Hartley noncommunist affidavit. On the eve of the election, the Company fired 200 UE supporters—shop stewards, local officers, and rank-and-file members. The election results were predetermined. (It wasn't until 1980 that Stewart-Warner workers were able to come back to UE after suffering great losses in earnings and worsened working conditions.) . . .

In 1952, 30,000 employees of International Harvester represented by UE in Chicago and several other midwestern cities struck against company-demanded wage cuts. Their burden in a strike that lasted several months was made more difficult by the miraculous appearance of the UnAmerican Activities Committee in Chicago to "investigate" Communism in the labor movement.

In the next several years, the entire government machinery was involved in the drive to make good, even if belatedly, on GE's "kill 'em in 1949" program. In city after city, where the IUE as well as a number of other CIO and AFL unions hungered for a piece of the UE membership, the Board would order an election, and a congressional or state UnAmerican Committee would appear on the scene to subpoena UE leaders and rank-and-file members on the eve of an election to question them for the benefit of the headlines, the raiders, and the companies. John F. Kennedy,

Hubert Humphrey, and a number of others with liberal pretensions addressed public meetings on such occasions.

In late 1953 the UE petitioned for an election at the big Lynn, Massachusetts, GE plant, where it had lost by a narrow margin during a Red-baiting orgy three years earlier.

A few weeks before the scheduled election at this plant, the local daily newspaper said:

> Coming almost simultaneously with the Washington decision was an announcement in New York last night by Sen. Joseph R. McCarthy (R-Wis) that he and his Senate Investigating Committee will hold a closed hearing in Boston tomorrow at 11:00 A.M. on security policies and alleged Communist infiltration at GE's Lynn and Everett plants.

One day before the election, the company announced what came to be known as the Cordiner Doctrine after the company president, Ralph Cordiner. GE announced that "it will immediately . . . suspend employees who refuse to testify under oath . . . when queried in public hearings conducted by competent government authority."

The Bill of Rights would no longer apply to GE employees.

Of course, the "testimony" by informers and the badgering of witnesses by McCarthy was immediately leaked to the press for headlines as workers went to vote.

Despite all this, the UE was defeated in that election by a mere couple of hundred votes among 13,000 employees.

Questions

1. Was it an injustice to drive the UE out of these plants just because they were led by communists? Why or why not?
2. Are the political beliefs of union leaders a legitimate subject for potential union members to consider in a union election?
3. What interest might the federal government have had in eradicating the UE?

John F. Kennedy Questions Jimmy Hoffa about Union Ethics, 1957

In 1957 Senator John L. McClellan of Arkansas created a committee to examine corruption in both the labor and management sides of collective bargaining. It came, however, to concentrate on a few corrupt unions, especially the International Brotherhood of Teamsters. The committee discovered instances where union officials misused funds, hired armed thugs to attack their enemies, and committed extortion. The main result of the hearings was the 1959 Landrum-Griffin Act, which regulated the internal affairs of trade unions and guaranteed union members a variety of rights.

James Hoffa, then a business representative and Vice President of the International Brotherhood of Teamsters, became the embodiment of union corruption during these televised hearings. Despite testimony such as the following, Hoffa became president of the Teamsters union later in 1957. He was convicted of jury tampering in 1964 and began serving time in prison for this offense in 1967. Released from prison in 1971 after President Richard Nixon commuted his sentence, he disappeared in 1975 while plotting a comeback. No trace of him has ever been found.

During the McClellan Committee hearings, questioning by the Massachusetts Senator and future president John F. Kennedy established that a trucking company with which the Teamsters bargained did business and made payments to a firm owned in part by Hoffa's wife. Here, Hoffa defends this relationship:

Excerpt from United States Senate, Select Committee on Improper Activities in the Labor or Management Field, "Hearings Before the Select Committee on Improper Activities in the Labor or Management Field," Part 13, 85th Congress, First Session, 1957, 4950–51.

Mr. HOFFA . . . Senator, I find nothing wrong with a labor representative having a business or his family having a business that may be in the same industry that that particular union has organized, because it has been my experience that if you can be corrupt for a very small amount of money or a very large amount of money, there isn't much difference. My record speaks for itself, and my contracts speak for themselves, that they are equivalent to anything that has been negotiated in any industry without strikes, Senator.

Senator KENNEDY. The only thing I am talking about, Mr. Hoffa, is the fact that, for a $4,000 investment [by your wife], a profit of over $125,000 was made. There certainly was an intimate business relationship between you and a major employer. I am just wondering whether you, as a prominent labor leader, feel that it is proper for you to have, or labor leaders in general to have, such a relationship with men whom they are bargaining with collectively on behalf of their employees.

Mr. HOFFA. Senator, I will answer that by saying this: that I have been around a long time, and I know my employers probably better than most people know their employers who represent employees, and I have never made it a practice of trying to distinguish employers from employees other than at the bargaining table, and I find nothing objectionable if an employer is going to lease equipment from someone who is not a stranger, providing there is no strings attached to that particular investment.

However, I notice that the ethical practices committee [of the AFL-CIO*] has placed certain rules and regulations concerning investments and, as rapidly as possible, even though I don't agree, I am disposing of everything that I own except what I will earn from the union, to comply with the ethical practices rulings.

However, I want to make it clear that, since that rule came down—and it came down this year, if you will recall—we have been attempting to sell this particular company. But, the money market being as tight as it is, it is rather difficult, without taking a loss, to sell at this particular time.

But, as rapidly as possible, that concern and my other businesses will be liquidated to the extent that I will be able to say, as

*The AFL-CIO expelled the Teamsters for corruption in December 1957.

some labor leaders like to say, and I don't, that management is wrong and I can have no part of it. I will simply say that, to comply with ethical practice, I will dispose of any holdings we have outside my personal property that I own, to comply with ethical practices rulings, even though I don't agree with them.

Senator KENNEDY. I am glad to hear that, Mr. Hoffa. It is not a question of management being wrong. It is just a question of whether a labor leader who is negotiating contracts should have an intimate business relationship of the kind that you have had with people whom he is obliged to negotiate with over the bargaining table.

Mr. HOFFA. I probably—

Senator KENNEDY. I think that is the reason that the AFL-CIO ethical practices [committee] thought that it involved a conflict of interest and should not be permitted.

Mr. HOFFA. Well, Senator Kennedy, I would say to you that, if a person owning a controlling interest in a business, I would believe without question, you would not need that rule to find that it was wrong. But I believe that, if there is a uniformity of payment for what the particular equipment is leased for, and the contracts speak for themselves in the matter of handling grievances, in the matter of keeping the equalization of wages in line with other industries, it should not be construed as being some sort of illegal operation or an untouchable operation, because it is my firm belief as a labor leader that, if you know the business you are negotiating in, and if you have some touch of responsibility, you will be in a better position at the bargaining table to get more for your men when it comes time to bargain.

My experience of knowing what can be produced out of trucks, by leasing equipment and paying union wages, has saved our drivers throughout the entire central conference from having any strikes and [made them] able to get at the same time the prevailing wage scales, prevailing increases, in many instances much higher and better fringe benefits, than the average union that takes the position that they don't want to know what the employers' business is about.

Senator KENNEDY. The ethical practices committee of the AFL-CIO took the opposite position, Mr. Hoffa, and I think for very good reason. But I am glad to hear that you are going in that category to go along with them.

QUESTIONS

1. Explain why Hoffa's business dealings had the potential to hurt Teamsters members.
2. Assuming Hoffa is right that his "contracts speak for themselves," does that make his dealings with employers more acceptable? Does this explain why Teamsters members tolerated apparent corruption in their union?
3. Was it right to impose restrictions on the activities of every union in the United States just because a few unions like the Teamsters operated in an unethical manner?

48

George Meany Testifies in Favor of Civil Rights Bills, 1963

In the years following World War II, union leaders found themselves working in close partnership with civil rights leaders. Both civil rights and collective-bargaining rights had the potential to give increasingly urban African-American workers the ability to share in the national prosperity of the postwar era. At the same time, the opponents of the civil rights movement were the same conservative southern Democrats who promoted laws that hampered union organizing.

In Senate testimony on what would eventually become the landmark Civil Rights Act of 1964, AFL-CIO president George Meany admits that some union locals resisted civil rights, but he emphasizes the national federation's interest in promoting full equality and full employment.

AMERICANS ALL OVER the United States have been awakened to the new urgency in the field of civil rights. The President has urged upon the Congress a new and vital civil rights program. And those in both the Senate and the House who stand for human rights have been given new strength to press for positive action.

I want to particularly commend the authors of the bills which are before you today, Senators Joseph Clark, Clifford Case, and Hubert Humphrey. These men have long been recognized for their stanch [sic] support of civil rights legislation and their ef-

Excerpt from *Hearings before the Subcommittee on Employment and Manpower of the Committee on Labor and Public Welfare, United States Senate,* 88th Cong., 1st sess., on S. 773, S. 1210, S. 1211, and S. 1937, July 24, 25, 26, 29, 31; August 2 and 20, 1963, 150–152.

forts to secure equality of opportunity for all Americans. That we are here today is another tribute to their unceasing efforts.

Mr. Chairman, the AFL-CIO supports strong Federal action in the areas President Kennedy outlined in his civil rights message of June 19. We believe that advances are long overdue in eliminating discrimination and segregation in the fields of voting, education, housing, and public accommodations.

But I must point out to the Congress that in the last three of these areas, true equality of opportunity cannot come about for our deprived minorities without equality of access to employment.

The Negro needs money to keep his children in school.
The Negro needs money to purchase decent housing.
The Negro needs money to utilize public accommodations.
And the only way he can get that money is to find a good job.

So, it seems plain to us that most of the rights we seek to insure for our minority groups depend on our ability first, to create jobs, and second, to assure their availability on a nondiscriminatory basis for all.

The first of these prerequisites has been a matter of vital concern to Government, labor, and industry for a long time. For more than 5 years, unemployment in this country has exceeded 5 percent of the labor force.

In my statement to the President on the occasion of his meeting with labor leaders on June 13, I pointed out that "equal opportunity has meaning only if there is full opportunity for all." Without full opportunity, both Negroes and whites will suffer from inadequate education, poor housing, and inability to enjoy public accommodations.

Congress and the Administration must do their utmost to reduce unemployment to a reasonable level, for without full employment jobs for all Negroes cannot be had no matter how fair our employment practices.

We have urged the Congress again and again to pass a program of tax cuts to increase consumer purchasing power, programs of public works in a variety of fields to create jobs directly, and expanded manpower retraining, vocational education, and all the other programs designed to create jobs and to qualify people to fill them.

We assume that Congress will meet its responsibilities in this area, and that America will move toward full employment.

That is one part of the problem. The other part is Federal action to insure equal opportunity.

Much has already been done in this area, by the Federal Government, by State and local governments, by employers, and by labor unions.

But much remains to be done by all these groups if we are to attain the democratic goal of equality for all in these United States.

Let me repeat to you what I have said many times before: the trade union movement stands strongly for civil rights, but we know we have civil rights problems within our own ranks.

I spoke earlier about the long and continuing support which the AFL-CIO and its predecessors have given to civil rights legislation. The resolutions which established this policy have repeatedly been adopted on the floor of our conventions.

But we know there are those who in fact dissent. We know this through their actions at the local union level, which we deplore.

For this reason, the AFL-CIO has worked diligently to eliminate segregation, not only in our unions, but in all of American life. Our Civil Rights Committee, and our staff department of civil rights, have made great strides.

Cooperating with our affiliated international unions, State, and local central bodies, they have done much all over the country, in the South as well as in the North, to end discriminatory practices in unions.

They cannot hope to be wholly successful, however, simply because the AFL-CIO has only limited powers, and certainly has no manpower to police all of the 60,000 local unions of our affiliates.

But more important, ours is not a monolithic organization; it is a confederation of autonomous unions. The only sanction we can use against a union is to expel it from our organization.

And if we expel a union, we have done nothing to eliminate its discriminatory policies. Indeed, we may only succeed in freezing these policies.

This is one reason why we want strong Federal legislation, legislation putting the muscle of Federal law behind the goal of equal opportunity. We need the power of the Federal Government to do what we are not fully able to do ourselves.

QUESTIONS

1. To what extent does Meany take responsibility for unions' mixed records on civil rights? To what extent does he deny responsibility?
2. What evidence does he give of the labor movement's commitment to civil rights?
3. Given Meany's comments, why did some union locals oppose civil rights?

49

Mike Hamlin on Black Workers' Disputes with the United Auto Workers, 1970

Although AFL-CIO unions were a big part of the post–World War II civil rights coalition, many African Americans found fault with union leaders' priorities. While unemployment rates hit historic lows nationally, unemployment remained widespread in black communities, especially in industrial cities like Detroit. At a time when antidiscrimination laws and voting rights laws sought to atone for centuries of official racism, the labor movement's officially race-blind, class-based approach to social change often appeared to condone past racism.

In Detroit auto plants in the summer of 1968, these tensions boiled over, as black workers at Dodge and Chrysler plants staged wildcat strikes to protest job classifications that remained grounded in racial discrimination and the national union's unwillingness to address grievances specific to black workers. Leaders of the first of the wildcat strikes organized the Dodge Revolutionary Union Movement (DRUM), which inspired more radical caucuses in auto plants. These caucuses fused as the short-lived League of Revolutionary Black Workers. Although UAW leaders pointed out their union's role in integrating auto factories in the 1930s, many black workers in the late 1960s saw these efforts as "coasting" thirty years later.

LEVIATHAN: Mike, you said that [black workers] came to you as a last resort. I take it that they were in UAW locals. How did the UAW deal or not deal with the problems that these black workers

Excerpt from Jim Jacobs and David Wellman, "An Interview With Ken Cockrel and Mike Hamlin of the League of Revolutionary Black Workers," in *'Our Thing is DRUM.'* Reprinted from *Leviathan* 2:2 (June, 1970), 12–14.

had which left them no alternative but to turn to a more revolutionary direction?

Mike: Well, let's look at it this way. When I was younger I worked at Ford's in the stamping plant. I worked for six weeks and then the lay-off came. So I began to look for a job. You have to understand that there's a grapevine in the black community that tells you where people are being hired on a given day. And if I was circulating in the same set that I was at the time, I could probably tell you today where they're hiring people. It gets around all over the city. When you show up there, you see the long lines of the same people that you saw the day before at Ford, or the day before at Cadillac's or whatever. So there's these long lines and you go there and stand and they hire a few people and then they send the rest of them away. Now, what happens is there may be two or three whites in that line. And once you get into the employment office, they may hire a large number of blacks and a few whites.

But then you go in and see what kind of jobs they're giving. The whites generally get the easy jobs: inspection or jobs on small stock. The blacks go in and get the heavy jobs, the hard jobs, and the dangerous jobs. The reason for that is kind of interesting. First of all, whites won't work on those kinds of jobs. That's a fact. In plants where blacks are in the majority, for example, the Ford engine plant in Dearborn, the line runs at a back-breaking pace. The same operation in another Ford engine plant, where there is a majority of white workers, the line runs, you know, at the agreed upon rate. In the Mahwah, New Jersey Assembly Plant, the line runs at 52 units an hour. And it doesn't vary because the work force is 80 percent white. If they speed it up, the white workers are going to walk out. But they know that we are so uptight for jobs, and there's such a large supply of reserve labor, black labor, cheap labor available for them, that they can speed it up on us as much as they want to. And if we quit, they can always bring somebody in at the new rate. So in the Mahwah plant, they run 52 units an hour. In the Ford plant here, the agreed upon rate is something like 64. But in actuality, the line goes up to 76 in certain instances, depending on whether or not the foreman is meeting his quota, or whether or not he thinks he can slip one over on the workers.

Leviathan: What's the union agreement about productivity?

Mike: At the Ford Dearborn I think it's 64. But it doesn't mean anything because, first of all, when you're working there, you're working so hard, the line's going so fast that you're not counting. And secondly the union is not counting. The union has no power and no real concern about controlling that line. If the foreman can get away with it without the workers knowing that, then that's cool. What happens is, the workers can tell when they get really ridiculous because you're working so fast. And, like, some lines, you know, go on several floors. And sometimes a guy will be trying to run downstairs. He gets so far behind he'll be trying to run downstairs trying to catch up with the cars that he's supposed to be working on. So, that's why those departments are overwhelmingly black in almost every instance. The same applies for the foundry where work is dirty and dangerous, and a lot of workers get lung diseases. Little's done about it.

We also found out in certain instances, like last summer during the time of economic boom, that the guys were being rotated from plant to plant. They would hire a lot of people, keep them for 89 days since you're on probation 90 days, and the 89th day, you're discharged and you had to go to another plant. So this inflated the employment figures. In actuality, what they're doing was rotating guys from plant to plant. They fire them on various charges, trumped-up charges. At Ford Rouge they would fire six hundred workers per week. You know, six hundred workers per week. I mean that's every week. And at the Dodge Main plant they were firing 300 per week. And at Eldon they were firing 300 a week. And none of those people ever got back. They didn't even bother to fight. First of all, those who have 89 days don't have any recourse: they're not in the union even though they paid the initiation fees and paid dues for those three months. But they don't have full union rights. And then the other people are people who are "undesirable" people. At that time they were firing them for Afro hairdos, you know, or for any sign of militancy or any kind of resistance to the harassment that was going on.

Before we came along they were constantly intimidating the workers, constantly threatening them with being fired, giving them time off and that kind of thing. They always had them in a state of intimidation, in a state of fear. And in certain instances,

we have reversed that. It's now the foremen and the labor relations people who are intimidated, who are afraid to do the kind
of things that they did before. And I think that's going to be the
pattern throughout these plants as we continue to organize.

But, you know, the actual individual foremen were bold on
the line: calling them names and walking up and kicking them.
Up until that time there were not too many instances, excepting
at the Ford Foundry, of people actually hurting or jumping on
the foremen and killing 'em or anything like that. Ford has always been so bad that the foundry has a history of supervisors
and union stewards getting killed and a few white workers too.
They'd come up and tell some guy: "you're not catching them
fast enough, speed up the line," you know and trying to get at
them that way. I mean if they're going to speed it up, at least
they don't have to add insult to injury. Come up and start talking
about kicking you in the behind or something if you don't keep
up. So that has been changed in Dodge. It still exists at Ford. . .

These kinds of things resulted in actions like a number of
wildcat strikes, which resulted in a number of people being fired.
One of the wildcat strikes which involved black and white workers ended up with all of the workers going back except one of the
founders of DRUM. But he continued working on the executive
committee of the League.

Besides the strikes, an organization was formed called the "Concerned Unionists" which was a caucus but which was doomed to
failure because the union apparatus was unresponsive. There was
nothing being done about any of these abuses being heaped on the
workers. So after they had gone all these routes, they didn't have
any other option but to come seek an alliance with us and an involvement with us. One of the mistakes that we did not make was
to set ourselves apart from the workers. What we did in fact was to
involve ourselves and integrate ourselves with the workers.

QUESTIONS

1. How would you summarize the relationship between race,
   work assignment, and the UAW?
2. Why didn't the UAW act on the complaints workers made?
3. How does the story of the LRBW resemble the history of other
   late-1960s social movements?

Working-Class Culture

Office workers. Courtesy Walter P. Reuther Library, Wayne State University.

"Judith Ann" on Life in "The Secretarial Proletariat"

So far, we have considered many kinds of women workers in this book. However, only after World War II did women begin to enter the white-collar work force in large numbers. In the years before feminism and the Civil Rights Act of 1964 (which, in part, made job discrimination on the basis of gender illegal), women office workers still faced difficult working conditions and limited opportunities compared to their male colleagues.

Judith Ann worked for a large insurance company in the early 1960s. Although not strictly secretarial, her job as a rater (one who determines the rates that policy holders would pay for their insurance) was entirely clerical. Here, she describes her work and the coping strategies that she and her female colleagues developed to get through the day.

THE WORKING DAY was from 8:00 A.M. to 4:00 P.M. We had to be in our seats with our coats hung up by eight sharp, when a bell rang to start us to work. We were allowed to start cleaning up at 3:35, and then we sat at clean desks with purses in hand from 3:45 to 4:00, when the bell rang again and we bolted the building. We had a short coffee break about half-way through the morning, and then 45 minutes for lunch. (The work day was thus officially $7^1/_4$ hours long; we were not paid for lunch period.) Since the whole floor went to lunch at the same time, it was easily and duly noted if you were even one minute late getting back. On paydays (every

Excerpt from "Judith Ann," "The Secretarial Proletariat," in Robin Morgan, ed. *Sisterhood is Powerful* (New York: Vintage Books, 1970), 88–90. Copyright © 1970 by Judith Ann.

other Friday) we got an extra half-hour for lunch—a state law so that employees could go to the bank. Paydays were also special because of the "quarter pool." This was voluntary, of course, but each payday nearly every employee on our floor put a quarter in the pool and his name in the hat. I played the quarter pool every payday I was there, and although I never won, I spent a lot of time planning what I would do with the approximately fifteen dollars if I ever did win. The quarter pool, the World Series, and an astronaut voyage (a few people brought in transistor radios and were allowed to play them very quietly the morning of the splash-down) were the only breaks in our routine.

We went to the ladies' room in groups of two or three, twice a day, after coffee break and again in the middle of the afternoon. Talking (in low tones and small quantities) with co-workers was allowed only with the neighbors directly to the side or front or back—even cater-corner was not permitted. (This rule applied to coffee break as well.) The atmosphere was similar to that of elementary school. We were even called "girls," not women, no matter what our ages. We had no rights, only duties. Each employee was allowed five sick days per year; after that you were docked—or fired. There was no severance pay.

The work itself was completely routinized, mindless toil. You got a stack of policies in the morning and you spent the day referring to a set of rate schedules and computing the rates on a Calculator—an adding machine that also multiplies and divides. Your work was then checked by a co-worker and rechecked by a supervisor, and then sent out to the typists. The typists were somewhere on another floor; I never found out where for sure. Typing was even more lowly than rating, so a rater never even met, much less mingled with the typists.

The isolation by hierarchy of the different levels of female clerical labor (secretaries, raters, typists, file clerks, in that order) was a very potent tool in the hands of management. By giving some units a sense of false privilege and all units feeling a rivalry with their sisters, we were effectively kept from any cross-unit solidarity or even sympathy, which would have been very threatening indeed to management.

Within the rating unit itself, however (and I suppose it was the same all over), there was a very warm feeling among the workers. Particularly the young unmarried raters developed strong friendships with each other and we often spent time together after working hours. We all hated our jobs, hated our supervisors, and spent long hours bitching about the conditions and plotting when and how we would quit. We also talked about what kind of jobs we would get instead—it was universally agreed that a small office with several men and only one or two girls would be a vast improvement over the rows and rows of women and the female supervisor that we now had to deal with. My friend Ann did leave while I was there. She went to an insurance agent's office. It was a small office, and she was clerical assistant to the three or four salesmen; in the insurance world, this was the *crème de la crème* of female employment, and the rest of us back at the old job were very envious.

The other subject we talked about even more consistently was men. Of course, we assumed that all this talk about "better jobs" was only conditional on our single status, and it was our firm belief that at the end of all present suffering lay the final reward: marriage. We talked and thought about men constantly. If an unmarried underwriter looked at one of us cross-eyed, we would discuss the implications for an entire lunch hour. If one of us got a letter from a boy (usually in the Service or away at college) or, glory be, had a date, it provided us with conversation for days. Two or three of the girls were engaged and we discussed their wedding plans—and the terrifying, glorious "first night"—daily. We were all virgins, and the repressed sexuality of these vibrant young girls was almost tangible in the atmosphere. Since the work was so routinized, I found myself able to indulge in sexual fantasies eight straight hours a day—a vast improvement over the quality of my fantasies during exams at college, because, since here I could do my work at the same time, there was less anxiety attached to them. This is in fact one of the most oppressive aspects of female clerical work: since the working conditions were so bad and our daily life so dull, the only bright spots in our lives were our relationships or hoped-for relationships with men. We sought refuge from our oppression as working women in the male supremacist institutions of dating and marriage, and in escapist consumerism of make-up and pretty clothes.

QUESTIONS

1. In what ways was the culture of these women workers different from the culture of men who might have worked similar jobs? In what ways was it the same?
2. How much of the "oppression" of these workers is because of their gender and how much is because they were working class?
3. If their jobs were so awful, why did women like Judith Ann choose to work at all?

51
Fred Cook Reports on
Hardhats vs. Hippies, 1970

So much of the history of American labor has assumed close connections between workers and the American left. However, the Vietnam War and the movement against it in the late 1960s created a deep divide between these two groups. Many workers were themselves veterans of World War II, and they identified with the anticommunist aims of the war. Furthermore, unlike in World War II, the bulk of those serving in the U.S. armed forces in the Vietnam War came from working-class families.

Although these tensions primarily simmered within families and in other private spheres, occasionally working-class resentment of the antiwar movement suffered in public. The most famous of these events were the so-called hard-hat riots of May 1970, in which New York City construction workers attacked antiwar marchers in lower Manhattan, with police largely looking on. The "hard-hats" proceeded to chant slogans against New York's liberal Republican mayor, John Lindsay, even attacking city officials who tried to order the mob away from City Hall. The actions of the "hard-hats" seemed to validate President Nixon's approach to the war.

In this article, investigative journalist Fred J. Cook argues that the "hard-hat" demonstrations were hardly spontaneous. Cook traces how ultra-right wing American politicians acted with the tacit approval of the New York City Police Department and a full endorsement from the leadership of the local building trades council and the national AFL-CIO.

Excerpt from Fred J. Cook, "Hard Hats: The Rampaging Patriots." Reprinted with permission from the June 15, 1970 issue of *The Nation*, pp. 712–719.

The man who tells this story has credentials of credibility. "I'm a veteran," he says, "and I believe in the flag, too. But I can't go along with all this stuff." . . . What follows is an account of the action as he saw it.

> The men left their jobs and marched up Broad Street. The police were already there. I was standing behind the police lines myself, and I saw what happened. All of a sudden flags broke out every-where, and handbills appeared as if by magic. They were being dis-tributed by this guy from the *New York Graphic*, and he had some helpers with him. When you saw that happen, you knew that this had to be a planned thing.
>
> What made me sick was the police. The kids were already spread all over the steps of the old Treasury building and the police lines were out in front. The fellows came marching up and were stopped by the police. Then they began to shove up against the police lines. They were pushing, pressing, and not a night stick was raised in anger. Suddenly the whole left side of the police line just melted away, and those yellow hats charged up the steps and began to beat up students.

In fairness to the police, says one long-time observer of the cops in action, there were probably several reasons for the police collapse on Bloody Friday. . . . "Yes, the police were warned in advance, but remember, nothing like this has ever happened be-fore and no one could conceive the scope of this thing. It was much like the time Watts went up in flames. People said in shock, 'Why, they're burning their own houses!' And so here the reac-tion was, 'Why, they are actually beating up people!' Then, too, a lot of cops have the same thoughts and emotions about demon-strators that the hard-hats have, and there may have been this reluctance to beat up a brother. I think the police, despite the warnings, were caught by surprise at what they had on their hands, but I doubt if there was any collusion, any prior understanding between police and hard-hats." . . .

As the hard-hats continued to claim the center of the stage, questions arose. What was behind these demonstrations? What forces in union ranks had led to the Bloody Friday outbreak? What impelled the unions to keep up the pressure? The answers are to be found on two levels—the low level of the ordinary construction worker, the high level of union leadership. As for the first, one observer comments:

> A lot of these guys feel they have legitimate grievances. They are almost the only segment of the population government hasn't paid much attention to. People whom they feel beneath them, the blacks and Puerto Ricans, for instance, demonstrate and get attention. The college kids, the more violent of them, spit on the flag and burn buildings; others demonstrate and cause upheavals—and they, too get attention. These construction men got the feeling they were in a kind of limbo, with nobody paying much attention to them. Obviously, there is a lot of frustration here.
>
> Then, remember that a lot of workers who were demonstrating against Lindsay don't even live in New York. In one union a good 40 per cent of the men working here, in another at least one-third, are not New Yorkers at all. They come here from Tennessee, from the Carolinas and Pennsylvania. Why? Because most of the high construction jobs in the nation are in New York . . . and [construction workers] belong to unions that are predominantly white. Some unions are all white . . . and there has been enormous pressure from minority groups, from government and from John Lindsay himself to open up the union rolls. It was no secret to these men that John Lindsay is determined to do all he can to open up these kinds of jobs to minorities in this town.

Considered especially threatening by the building trades was the [Nixon] Administration's "Philadelphia Plan" that would compel the hiring of fixed percentages of minority people.

Such was the situation when President Nixon extended the war into Cambodia and precipitated a national crisis . . . [so] the President turned for support to one source that has never failed the military-industrial complex—the leadership of George Meany, president of the AFL-CIO. On May 12. . . . Meany let it be known that he was 100 per cent behind the Administration in its Cambodian adventure.

Following this soul meeting, the New York building trades made the hard-hat demonstrations official policy. [Building and Construction Trades Council of Greater New York president] Peter Brennan circulated a letter to building trades councils throughout the nation, outlining his plans and urging them to spread the hard-hat demonstrations nationwide. . . .

[O]n Wednesday, May 20, almost every major construction project in Manhattan was shut down, and the hard-hats and their cohorts, in a sea of flags and banners, massed more than 100,000 strong around City Hall. This huge turnout was pictured on television and in the press as a spontaneous demonstration of patriotism, but it was nothing of the sort. It was a command performance.

Here is how it looked to one union man who *had* to march:

> After that Friday rally where there was so much violence, the union leadership evidently started to worry about the reaction. The word came down to cut out the rough stuff.
>
> The word was passed around to all the men on the jobs the day before. It was *not* voluntary. You *had* to go. You understand these are all jobs where the union controls your employment absolutely. If you're on a job where there's a lot of overtime and you stand in well with your shop steward, you get the overtime. If you make trouble, you're shifted to a job where there is no overtime—or maybe you don't get any job at all.
>
> We were told that if we got back to the job a half-hour after the parade ended, we'd be paid for a full day's work. Of course, the parade lasted until 3:30 and by the time the guys got back, the day was done. But everybody got paid.

That raises the question. The unions could order the men to march, but the unions don't pay them—the contractors do. "Sure," says this union man. "That in itself shows there had to be collusion somewhere."

To express his gratitude to the hard-hat super-patriots, the President called Peter Brennan and twenty-two other union leaders to the White House on Tuesday, May 26. They sat around the President's giant new Cabinet table and discussed the affairs of the nation for forty-seven minutes. Then the President held still while Brennan presented him with a hard-hat and pinned an American flag in his lapel.

The only sign of embarrassment at the White House was that the television camera crews and press photographers were not allowed to record the historic hard-hat crowning of the President of the United States.

QUESTIONS

1. Do you accept Cook's arguments? Why or why not?
2. Assuming the hard-hat demonstrations were orchestrated, do you think most participants resented having to participate, or did they welcome the chance to do so?
3. Consider this excerpt from the perspective of AFL-CIO president George Meany. How would you answer this article's accusations and perspective?

52

Ben Hamper on Coping with Life in an Automobile Factory

The 1980s dealt a near-fatal blow to the economy of factory towns in much of the United States, especially in cities that depended on the auto industry. Flint, Michigan, the home of the Buick division of General Motors, saw unemployment rates rise to 25 percent during the decade, as the combination of outmoded design of American cars and the anti-union policies of the Reagan administration fundamentally altered the taken-for-granted status of auto plants in America's Rust Belt.

Flint native Michael Moore, former publisher of independent newspapers in Flint and Lansing, made a darkly comic documentary on Flint's demise in 1989. Called Roger and Me, *the film showed Moore's pursuit of the president of General Motors, Roger Smith, as a metaphor for autoworkers trying to make sense of what happened to their way of life in the 1980s. Although seasoned observers of Flint in the 1980s and some film critics chastised Moore's ahistorical rendering of the plant shutdowns, Moore's film struck a popular nerve as the recession of the late 1980s began, and it became one of the highest-grossing documentary films of all time.*

Riding Moore's coattails was Ben Hamper, a Flint autoworker who had contributed concert reviews, cultural commentary, and slices of "shoprat" life to Moore's Flint Voice *and* Michigan Voice *newspapers. Hamper made a brief appearance in Moore's film; at that time, he was living at a psychiatric hospital, trying to recover from the panic attacks that led to his quitting work in GM plants.*

Excerpt from *Rivethead: Tales of the Assembly Line* by Ben Hamper. © 1991 by Ben Hamper. By permission of Warner Books.

Dead rock stars are singin' for me and the boys on the Rivet Line tonight. Hendrix. Morrison. Zeppelin. The Dead Rock Star catalogue churnin' outta Hogjaw's homemade boom box. There's Joplin and Brian Jones and plenty of Lynyrd Skynyrd. Dead Rock Stars full of malice and sweet confusion. Tonight and every night they bawl. The Dead Rock Stars yowling at us as we kick out the quota.

We're all here. Department 07, Blazer/Suburban Line—factory outpost FF-15 stenciled in black spray paint on the big iron girder behind Dougie's workbench. We're building expensive trucks for the General Motors Corp. We've come back once again to tussle with our parts and to hear the Dead Rock Stars harmonize above the industrial din.

The music of the Dead Rock Stars bursts from a ledge on Dougie's workbench—our hideaway for Hogjaw's stereo. Just before the start of every shift, Dougie goes through the complicated ritual of threading the cords and speaker wires from the stereo down a hollow leg in his workbench and into the plug at the base of the water fountain behind his job. The camouflage must be perfect. It is against company policy to use a General Motors electrical outlet as a source to summon up Dead Rock Stars. Only battery-powered radios are allowed.

Originally Hogjaw complied with this rule. It wasn't easy. Due to the enormous power demand of his radio creation, the Jaw was forced to lug a car battery into work with him every shift. You would see him strainin' his way through the parking lot every afternoon, a lunch bucket curled under one arm and his trusty Delco Weatherbeater hoisted on top of his other shoulder. Trailing behind him would be a couple of riveters with their arms locked around the speaker boxes—pallbearers bringin' around the tombs of the Dead Rock Stars.

This went on for a month or so before the security guards decided to halt the parade. Car batteries were declared illegal. Apparently the guards had concluded that it was a mighty dangerous precedent to allow workers to enter the plant premises with the batteries of their automobiles stashed on their shoulders. After all, whose heads would be in the vise if one of these sonic blasters pulled an overload up on the assembly line and spewed a load of battery acid into the eyes and ears of the screw brigade? Dead Rock Stars? Dead Shoprats? Not on *my* goddamn beat.

As for the popularity of Dead Rock Stars on the Rivet Line, I've settled upon this private theory. The music of the Dead Rock Stars is redundant and completely predictable. We've heard their songs a million times over. In this way, the music of the Dead Rock Stars infinitely mirrors the drudgery of our assembly jobs. Since assembly labor is only a basic extension of high school humdrum, it only stands to reason that the same wearied hipsters who used to dodge economics class for a smoke in the boys' room would later in life become fossilized to the hibernatin' soundtracks of their own implacable youth. Let the eggheads in economics have David Byrne and Laurie Anderson. The rivetheads be needin' their "Purple Haze" and "Free Bird" just like tomorrow needs today.

It's mob rule, and the mob demands Dead Rock Stars in their choir loft. Of course this arrangement provides for a fair amount of bitching from linemates in our area who hold no sacred allegiance to the songs of the rockin' deceased.

For example, there's Dick, the left-side rear spring man. He works directly across from Dougie, travelin' a nighly path that requires him to take the maximum dose of Dead Rock Star thud. It's nothing unusual to spot Dick takin' a deep drag from one of his ever-present Winstons while gazin' head-on into the boom box with this buggered glint in his eye and this twisted grimace on his face that almost pleads aloud for some kind of transistor malfunction, tweeter meltdown or any other variety of holy intervention.

Eddie and Jehan prefer rap music. On occasion, Jehan brings in his own battery-powered blaster and engages in this furious battle-of-the-blare with Hogjaw's almighty boom box. The Kings of Rap vs. The Dead Rock Stars vs. The Steady Clang of Industry. It makes for quite the raucous stew—sorta like pluggin' your head into the butt end of a Concorde during acceleration mode.

Management's stance on all this usually boils down to a simple matter of see no evil, hear no evil. If the guy in the tie can't actually see the visible evidence of how you're wastin' millions of corporate dollars, he's most often inclined to let the music flow. It keeps him off the hook. He doesn't have to play kill-joy. He can dummy up and pretend that that all those guitar solos he hears screechin' through the middle of the night are only happy by-products of a contented work force. His boss will love him, his wife will love him, his men will like him and the Company will somehow stagger on. Industry on the march. Bravo!

But even in victory, there's often a price to pay. Let us not forget that General Motors has already informed the work force that there won't be any profit sharing to spread around this year. Too much waste. Too many buyouts. Too few pennies. And I imagine those damn utility bills are way out of sight too.

Oh well, what can I say? I'm just sitting here waiting for the next chassis to arrive. I'm tapping my toes to the beat of the Dead Rock Stars. Ten feet to my right, I can hear the trickle of untold billions bein' sucked outta the corporate coffers through the base of the water fountain behind Dougie's workbench.

I'm thinking that rock stars, even dead ones, don't come cheap.

QUESTIONS

1. How does music play a similar role on the assembly line to other uses of music in the workplace? How is this instance different?
2. How does Hamper show contempt for his job? How does he show pride in it?
3. Find the examples of small-scale sabotage that Hamper discusses. Do you think that tactics like these are commonplace in modern American workplaces? Why or why not?

53

"Keffo" Lays Out Patterns of Temp Worker Solidarity, ca. 1997

The recession that lasted from the 1987 stock market crash through the early 1990s led to a reordering of the social contract in white-collar employment. Although white-collar workers avoided the cut-backs that threw millions of blue-collar workers out of jobs in the late 1970s and early 1980s, this recession led to huge dislocations.

In the workplace, many positions that had been filled with full-time employees were shifted to "temporary" positions. Employment agencies contracted with employers for temporary (temp) workers, who assumed positions at the bottom of the ladder at workplaces of all sorts. People working as temps hoped that they would have an inside track to full-time employment, but these hopes were infrequently realized and many temps sought other ways of coping with a no-future, no-benefits, working environment.

Keffo (Jeff Kelly), a long-time temp in Madison, Wisconsin, edited a self-published, photocopied magazine called Temp Slave *in the mid-1990s.* Temp Slave, *and other fly-by-night magazines like it around the country, ran stories of everyday sabotage and strategies for survival in a workplace that seemed to treat even college-educated, white-collar workers like disposable machinery. In this excerpt, Kelly discusses the limited power workers have in a postindustrial society.*

A TEMP WORKER has little or no rights in the workplace. In essence, a temp worker is close to being a nonentity. Sadly, nothing much can be done to alleviate the situation. A temp worker can be moved from job to job within a workplace, even though the temp may

Excerpt from *Best of Temp Slave!* edited by Jeff Kelly, published by Garrett County Press, (www.gcpress.com).

have been told they would do only one kind of job. As for job security, obviously there is none.

The normal avenues of channeling discontent about a job are not open to temps. For example, the normal course of unionizing a workplace is out of the question. Most companies set up Human Resource departments to act as a buffer between their workers and management. If a problem arises, the Human Resource managers are summoned to sort out the mess. But, this does nothing for temps since any overt complaints about a job by a temp will more than likely result in termination. Finally, getting unemployment benefits off a temp agency is like pulling teeth. Most of the time, requests for benefits are denied.

So, a temp is forced to put up and shut up or get out. However, there are a few things a temp can do to gain a semblance of power in the workplace.

First, DON'T SPEED UP! SLOW DOWN! Most of the time a temp is expected to work at the rate that a full-time worker does or faster. At first a temp may want to impress upon [their supervisors] the fact that they are capable of doing the job. But, once this is accomplished there is no reason for a temp to continue the pace. If you are working with a group of temps, band together and SLOW DOWN your rate of work. Slowing down your work allows your assignment to linger on longer. After all, why put yourself out of work? Plus, a group of temps working together cohesively puts the company [on] notice that people cannot be treated like slaves.

Second, NEVER rat on another temp to the bossman! Trying to put yourself above other temps is a silly and ultimately a hopeless thing to do. The person doing the ratting may think they are getting ahead, or think that the bossman will grant special favors, or think it will lead to a fulltime job. But it seldom ever does. What it does do is divide the workforce and keep people in place. To get rid of a rat, a few simple things can be done—"lose" their paperwork (make them look bad in the eyes of the bossman), chill out the rat (do not associate with the person on break time). And never volunteer to work with a rat if two people are needed for a job. In other words, make it known that they are not wanted in your work area.

Third, GET BACK AT THE BASTARDS! If you are being treated like shit by a company give it right back. Many companies entrust you with sensitive information. Use this info, "lose" it, sabotage it. Learn your job well and take every advantage possible with it.

Finally, if you are ending an assignment and really want to mess up the works legally, there is a fun thing you can do. Start talking union to everyone in the workplace. This gives you the opportunity to file charges with the National Labor Relations Board (NLRB). The NLRB is a national governmental agency set up to broker labor disputes. Under law, a worker is allowed to organize unions in the workplace. But, even with the law, workers are still fired. However, filing charges with the NLRB is a kick in the ass to a company because it forces them to deal with investigations and endless paperwork. In the best case scenario you may win your case and receive back pay sometimes amounting to thousands of dollars. But, even if you lose you can go away happy knowing that you were an incredible pain in the ass to the corporate hacks.

In closing, a workforce divided by petty jealousies, fear and self-loathing is a workforce that plays into the hands of the bosses. DON'T MAKE IT EASY FOR THEM! THEY DON'T DESERVE IT!

QUESTIONS

1. Is Kelly's call for sabotage and other kinds of resistance in the best interests of temp workers? Explain.
2. Why does Kelly have little faith that unions can help temp workers? Is he right? Explain.
3. The title of Kelly's 'zine implies that he equates temp work with slavery. To what extent do you think this comparison is valid? In what ways might it be overstated?

William Greider, from "One World, Ready or Not," 1997

One of the most important changes to take place in the American economy during the late twentieth century was the growth of the global marketplace. This has improved the prices available to American consumers as textiles made in Myanmar, toys made in China, or oranges grown in Brazil have become available in stores across the nation. It has also hurt American workers as many jobs that were once performed in the United States have been exported to other countries. Globalization allows manufacturers to save on wages—it also makes it easier for them to avoid unions.

Many of the plants now producing goods for the United States market hire unskilled, low-wage workers. In his book One World, Ready or Not, *journalist William Greider describes a visit to a different kind of factory, a microchip-manufacturing facility located in the southeast Pacific Asian nation Malaysia but owned by the American company Motorola. In many ways the plant is run just as it would be were it located in the United States, but at the same time the culture of the workers employed therein generates keen differences.*

IN THE INDUSTRIAL ZONE at Petaling Jaya outside Kuala Lumpur, a line of dingy blue buses began delivering workers for the 2 P.M. shift change at the Motorola plant. Motorola's blue logo was visible from the freeway, along with some other celebrated names of electronics like Canon, Sanyo, Panasonic and Minolta. Its factory looked like a low-slung office building facing an asphalt parking lot that was bordered by palms and giant yews. The white

Excerpt reprinted with the permission of Simon & Schuster from *One World, Ready or Not* by William Greider. © 1997 by William Greider.

facade was temporarily decorated with dozens of red paper lanterns and gilded banners in honor of Chinese New Year. Above the front entrance, a billboard invited workers to enter the "Motorola 10K Run," winners to compete at the U.S. Austin marathon.

The arriving workers passed through glass doors and headed down a long gleaming corridor toward the changing room, past the library and health center and an automatic banking machine. All of them were women, and most were young, small and delicate by American standards. They were dressed in the modesty of Islam—flowing ankle-length dresses, heads and shoulders draped by the Muslim *tundjung*, silken scarves of pale blue, orange and brown. A few wore the fuller, more conservative black veils that closely framed their faces like pale brown hearts and encased the upper body like shrouds.

"Good afternoon, ladies." Roger Bertelson, Motorola's country manager, was showing me around, and the two of us towered above the stream of women. They passed by, eyes down, barely nodding. Bertelson had brush-cut hair and a sunny American forwardness, like a taller version of Ross Perot. He was explaining the "I Recommend" board on the wall, a display covered with snapshots of employees who had made successful suggestions.

"We had to change the culture," Bertelson said, "because the Malay home does not encourage women to speak out. The daughter is supposed to have babies and take care of the husband. The idea was to break down the resistance to speaking out. We use positive reinforcement, just like you would work with schoolchildren. First, convince them that you are going to listen to them. Then have them stand up before their peers for recognition."

The automatic teller machine also disturbed the culture. "We had to change the pattern," he said. "She had to go home and tell her father: 'I'm not going to bring my money home in a pay envelope any more. It's going into the bank.'"

Farther along the hallway, the women passed by a collection of Norman Rockwell paintings—each accompanied by an inspirational aphorism in English. "People Will Take Note of Excellent Work." "You'll Be Prepared for Anything with Enthusiasm." "What We Say Is as Important as How We Say It." It was hard to know the meaning these homey American images might have in this setting.

At the changing room, the women removed shoes and veils and proceeded to the gowning room across the hall. A few minutes later they emerged cloaked in ghostly white jumpsuits, wearing surgical masks and hooded bonnets. They looked like otherwordly travelers, more chaste than they would appear in the most severe Islamic garments. At the air shower, blasts of purified air cleansed them of any remaining particles of dust. Then they entered the sealed operations room, where the rows of complex machines and monitors awaited the next shift.

Once inside, the women in space suits began the exacting daily routines of manufacturing semi-conductor chips. They worked in the realm of submicrons, attaching leads on devices too small to see without the aid of electronic monitors. Watching the women through an observation window, Bertelson remarked: "She doesn't really do it, the machine does it."

The manufacturing process for semiconductors literally bounced around the world. Larger silicon wafers that included the circuitry for multiple chips had been designed and fabricated back in the States (or perhaps in Scotland, where the industry had also located a major production base). Then the wafers were flown by 747 to Malaysia (or perhaps Singapore or the Philippines or elsewhere in Asia) for final assembly—sawed into individual chips, wired tested and packaged. The finished chips were shipped back to North America, Asia and Europe to become the functional guts of TV sets, computers, portable phones, missile control systems and countless other products.

The spectacle of cultural transformation at Motorola was quite routine—three times a day, seven days a week—but it conveyed the high human drama of globalization: a fantastic leap across time and place, an exchange that was banal and revolutionary, vaguely imperial and exploitive, yet also profoundly liberating. In the longer sweep of history, the social intrusions of modern technology might be as meaningful as the economic upheavals. Motorola and the other semiconductor companies settled in Malaysia have managed to unite the leading edge of technological complexity with shy young women from the *kampong*, rural villages where destiny was defined as helping peasant fathers and husbands harvest the rice or palm oil.

At lunch in the company cafeteria, Bertelson and his management staff talked about the complexity. "We improve our productivity 15 percent a year, that's company policy," he said. "We have a roadmap for each one of our operations that calls for a 10x improvement by the year 2000, by automating and improving worker efficiency. We will do that."

Malaysian production was not exempt from the same steep "learning curve" that drove price competition through the global industry, a standing assumption that costs and prices will fall by roughly 30 percent every time the volume doubles. To defend market share, every producer must continuously squeeze out more waste and imperfection or develop the new materials and production methods that could keep up with the curve. "Our technology, the miniaturization, is growing so fast that we really need to get the human element out of the process as fast as we can," Bertelson said.

Around the lunch table Bertelson's department managers looked like a visionary's ideal of multicultural cooperation. Chinese, Malay, Indian, black, yellow, pale brown, Christian, Buddhist, Muslim, Hindu. The only white guys were Bertelson and a Scottish engineer named Dave Anderson, hired from Singapore. Longinus Bernard, an Indian from Johore whose father had worked on colonial estates, described the early days in 1974 when Motorola started up. "We were so small, everybody knows everybody," he said. "it was really—how do you call it—a good feeling."

Hassim Majid, manager of government affairs, explained how the racial diversity had been achieved. "We were advised by the government to play an active role in restructuring the ethnic composition of the company," he said. "We were to hire x number of Malay people like me, Chinese and Indians, just like your affirmative action in the United States." Motorola did well in meeting the government requirement.

The Kuala Lumpur operations, Motorola's largest outside the United States, had 5,000 employees, 80 percent Malay and 3,900 ladies, as the managers called them. The company had plans to double this facility, though not its employment. It represented one of the ripe anomalies of global economic revolution: while conservative ideologues in America fiercely contested the threat of multiculturalism, conservative American corporations were out around the world doing it. In the global context, the preoccupation of American politics with race and cultural superiority seemed ludicrous, out of touch and perhaps also dangerous.

QUESTIONS

1. What aspects of the Malaysia plant seem uniquely American? What aspects seem to have been influenced by the culture of the workforce?
2. Why might Motorola have hired Malaysian women instead of Malaysian men for this job?
3. Do you think the opportunity to work at Motorola is a net benefit for Malaysian workers? Explain.